Women Who Changed Things

~· Linda Peavy & Ursula Smith ·~

Women Who Changed Things

CHARLES SCRIBNER'S SONS
New York

PHOTO CREDITS: p. 1, from *Fighting for Life* by Sara Josephine Baker (Arno Press, 1974); p. 23, Western History Collections, University of Oklahoma; p. 45, Courtesy of the Harvard University Archives; p. 61, Manuscript Department, William R. Perkins Library, Duke University; p. 79, Courtesy of University of Nebraska Press; p. 100, Chicago Historical Society; p. 121, Library of The American Alpine Club; p. 141, The Ida B. Wells Papers, Department of Special Collections, University of Chicago Library; p. 159, Mark Twain Memorial, Hartford, Connecticut.

Library of Congress Cataloging in Publication Data
Peavy, Linda S.
Women who changed things.
Summary: Presents biographies of nine women active
between 1880 and 1930 who made outstanding contributions
in the fields of medicine, religion, politics, business,
arts and letters, education, athletics, and social action.
Includes index.
1. Women—United States—Biography—Juvenile litera-
ture. 2. United States—Social conditions—1865–1918—
Juvenile literature. 3. United States—Social conditions
—1918–1932—Juvenile literature. [1. Biography.
2. United States—Social conditions—1865–1918. 3. United
States—Social conditions—1918–1932] I. Smith, Ursula.
II. Title.
HQ1412.P4   1983   920.72′0973   [920]   82–21612
ISBN 0–684–17849–4

3 5 7 9 11 13 15 17 19   F/C   20 18 16 14 12 10 8 6 4 2

Printed in the United States of America

For Ursula, Nora, and Erica

Contents

Preface

Conceived in the midst of research for another book, the idea for this collective biography was a happy accident born of an illuminating moment—the discovery that the passage of federal legislation regulating food additives was due, in large part, to the campaign launched and carried out by a single person, a New Jersey clubwoman whose name we had never heard before and have not seen since.

A rush of questions followed. How could such an accomplishment have been forgotten? How could her story have been neglected? And how many other such untold stories were there? How many other women had lived lives of quiet inspiration, directly and indirectly improving the lives of their fellows, yet never achieving the recognition their accomplishments warranted?

That very afternoon we began a list tentatively titled "Women Who Changed Things." The list grew slowly at first, then almost exponentially as our casual readings became obsessive research. We pored over the volumes of *Notable American Women*, searching for examples of women who changed things. The fascinating biographies summarized on the pages of that invaluable reference filled us with an awe for what had been accomplished by the women of our society, accomplished in quiet, often unassuming ways by strong and sensitive women who saw needs and would not be denied.

But these amazing accomplishments had gone largely unsung. Living in an era when fame and fortune were almost exclusively masculine prerogatives, many of these women had never enjoyed the recognition they deserved. Others had risen to brief fame, then slipped into obscurity. We were determined that their stories should be exhumed, investigated, and told in all their aspects.

But there was a myriad of stories to be told. In *Notable American Women* alone there are brief biographies of over 1300 subjects. And our friends and relations, upon hearing of our new fascination, each seemed to have his or her own candidate to add to our list. By this time we had found an editor who shared our enthusiasm for telling these stories, and the need to shape our still nebulous ideas into book proposal form forced us to make choices from the by now unwieldy list.

To begin the painful task of narrowing the field, we set criteria by which choices were to be made. Holding with our original idea, we decided that a subject must have demonstrably changed things— what she had set her mind and hand to must have had a significant effect on the lives of others, not only by directly improving the quality of life for her contemporaries but by opening new opportunities for people of succeeding generations. Further, the women we wrote about should be women whose stories had hitherto been largely neglected.

To give the work some sense of unity, we imposed a time frame. There seemed to be a feminist ferment beginning in the late nineteenth century and passing into quiescence shortly after the achievement of woman's suffrage. That 50-year span, from 1880 to 1930, not only seemed a particularly auspicious and exciting one for women's history but also happened to be our favorite period of American history. We decided to limit our subjects to American women whose effective work was, for the most part, accomplished within those chronological boundaries.

Still other considerations controlled our final choices. We were quite frankly concerned that our women represent the broad ethnic makeup and regional differences of the turn-of-the-century American population.

We were also mindful that there must be enough written documentation of each woman's work to enable us to tell her story as fully as possible. It was at this point that we lost Alice Lakey, the New Jersey clubwoman who fought against adulteration of foods and who first inspired us to search out the stories. In her case, and in others, it seemed highly unlikely that we could amass enough primary sources to flesh out a story.

We found a further focusing when we decided to designate certain fields of achievement and to choose a single woman to represent each field. Originally we chose the fields of politics, business, arts and letters, science, social action, education, religion, medicine, and athletics as fields representing vital areas of human involvement. But those fields obviously have blurred boundaries, and several of our subjects were active in more than one of them.

Given these blurrings, we chose the strongest representatives from each of the fields, judgment as to "strongest" always being colored by our own very personal preferences and prejudices. For instance, from the many candidates in the field of medicine, we chose Sara Josephine Baker—primarily because her penchant for questioning the unquestionable held for us a personal appeal. Unhampered by undue attention to shoulds and oughts, she brought about such wide-sweeping, lifesaving changes in public health care that she seemed an almost unbelievable achiever. Subsequent research broadened our view of her character and her accomplishments, yet did nothing to dispel the awe we had first felt for so strong a figure.

Once our final choices were made and we began to explore each life in depth, our initial perceptions of the subject almost invariably underwent subtle changes. As each woman became a fully dimensioned figure, she inevitably became a real person for us, and often a person far different from the one we had imagined. For example, Kate Barnard, our politician, almost didn't make our final list because we fretted over the obvious brevity of her active career. When further research revealed that mental and physical illness had caused her untimely departure from public life, we deemed this "weakness," an easy judgment that momentarily obscured the ultimate strength of the woman. Fortunately, her story was so compelling that it forced itself upon us, and we hope we have captured the courageous spirit of Kate Barnard, a woman who broke before she yielded.

We chose to tell Williamina Fleming's story because we were caught by the idea that an immigrant housemaid could compile such an astounding record as stargazer. However, the colorful personal story we had expected to find never materialized, and we were left with some intriguing, unanswered questions.

Orie Latham Hatcher drew our attention and made our list because the task she undertook was a task that we knew from our own background to be a monumental one. In the end, documenting her professional accomplishments and describing her efforts to change the attitudes of fellow Southerners proved to be far easier for us than finding out about the personal life of this intensely private person. Our curiosity concerning any close relationships she might have had remained largely unsatisfied.

Leta Stetter Hollingworth initially attracted us because she dared to test long-standing theories as to the innate inferiority of women, but our appreciation for her accomplishments grew as we discovered the Hollingworth who, as a troubled teen, was caught in the "fiery furnace" of an unhappy home and who, as a young wife, was barred by her gender from the professional world she had prepared herself to enter.

From among many women active in social work, we chose Mary McDowell, primarily because we liked a woman who exerted such a tangible, measurable impact upon the one small universe that was her neighborhood. And we were caught by her colorful titles. How could anyone not want to learn more about the "Settlement Lady," the "Garbage Lady," the "Duchess of Bubbly Creek," "Fighting Mary," "Aunt Mary," and the "Angel of the Stockyards"? We found behind the titles a woman with a multiplicity of interests, all centered on a single cause—the betterment of life "back of the yards."

We chose Annie Smith Peck because we identified strongly with one who let her sense of adventure outrun her sense of propriety. Our early fascination held as we followed Peck's colorful career as scholar and alpinist and came to realize that here was a woman who lived for challenge. She remained an enigma—a peripatetic with no discoverable supportive relationships, and more than a bit of a banty—yet she stands as a superb example of woman as athlete, testing her physical and psychic strength against dangerous odds. When we came upon Ida Wells-Barnett we knew we had to tell her story, not only because she amply filled our need to include a minority figure in our group but also because she would, by any measure, merit inclusion in a company of women who changed things. During our research we found ourselves at times put off by the violence of some of her actions and wondered whether a person seeking change through violence should have a place in this collection. But our readings and discussions brought a gradual appreciation of the vast difference in the emotional intensity involved in fighting against an evil directed against one's own person and family and the intensity involved in fighting for a cause in which one has no personal stake. Our awakened appreciation of that difference brought first an understanding and finally an acceptance of the militancy of Ida Wells-Barnett.

Candace Thurber Wheeler was our choice because we felt immediate rapport for one who came to a late-life vocation after nearly 50 fulfilling years as homemaker and mother. At the outset we had some reservations about whether we would be able to do justice to the story of a woman lauded for her excellence in embroidery and tapestry weaving, domestic arts in which we profess, at best, only a profound disinterest. Despite these early reservations, we found Candace Thurber Wheeler to be an intriguing woman whose motives and accomplishments commanded our respect and whose warmth was so compelling that we found ourselves reluctant to read her obituary in the *New York Times,* a notice that would make an historical fact of the death of a woman who was too close to lose.

Indeed, the closeness we felt toward each of our women made us agonize in admitting to unknowns and unknowables, in conceding that, lacking either the space or the information, we would not be able to portray all the whys and hows of each woman's story. For to tell the full story of Mary McDowell, Orie Hatcher, Leta Hollingworth, or Williamina Fleming would require the acquisition of letters, memoirs, and professional papers that may never come to light; to do justice to the story of Annie Peck or Kate Barnard would require fuller documentation and trained psychological insight; to tell that of Sara Josephine Baker, Candace Wheeler, or Ida Wells-Barnett would require the luxury of a full-length biography.

For now, this collection stands as a monument to 9 women who did, in fact, change American life. Researching their lives was an intoxicating experience that filled our days with obsessive study and exciting correspondence. We joyed in breakthrough discoveries and serendipitous connections. The Columbian Exposition, the famous Chicago World's Fair of 1893, affords a striking example of such a connection. Bit by bit we followed the converging paths that led 4 of our women to Chicago in 1893. Mary McDowell, then a resident of Hull House, no doubt visited the exposition's famed "White City" many times that summer and fall; Candace Wheeler was there as director of the New York State Exhibit in the Woman's Building; Williamina Fleming went to the fair to deliver a speech to an assembly of the Congress of Astronomy and Astrophysics. And, all the while, Ida Wells-Barnett stood outside the "White City," handing out brochures entitled "The Reason Why the Colored American is Not in the Columbian Exposition."

While the progressive unfolding of intriguing coincidences such as this provided keen excitement, we found equal pleasure in coming upon more subtle parallels among the lives of our women, parallels in background, personality, and style, both personal and professional. But as often as we found striking parallels in these areas we found also striking dissimilarities. Some of our women came from affluence, some from poverty; some were strongly influenced by their fathers, some by their mothers, grandmothers, or great aunts. Some were raised in religion-centered homes, none were strongly church-oriented as adults, but most were motivated by a social consciousness based on religious principles.

The form and level of their education varied, though all were markedly intelligent, and all studied, traveled, or lectured abroad. All were devoted to their work, some single-minded, others following diverse drummers. Five of the 9 women treated in this collection never married, one was divorced, and 3 had supportive husbands who either shared their vision or encouraged their involvement. The 3 who were mothers exhibited vastly different styles of mothering.

We fully expected to find that these women drew much of their strength from supportive friendships. Yet in several cases we were unable to document the existence of any close relationships and were forced to accept the possibility that some of these women gave no time to the development of friendship. They were cause-driven beings, aptly described by a phrase Orie Hatcher devised for herself: "one of those terrible Social nuisances, a woman with a work to accomplish, come what will."

History offers many examples of cause-driven women who centered their lives in their work. But women daring to combine career, marriage, and motherhood have primarily been a phenomenon of this century. Leta Hollingworth argued that women of her day who chose to balance these 3 interests were living experimental lives from which future generations could learn much.

In a sense, all 9 of the women represented in this collection lived experimental lives. They moved in circles where women had not moved before, questioned long-standing assumptions, and devised innovative solutions to old problems. We have only begun to tell their stories, and we can only speculate as to what else is to be found in their lives and in the lives of countless others. We leave off our work here, still needing to know more about these forgotten achievers and the many others like them, still gripped by the excitement of having been touched by these experimental lives.

Acknowledgments

*F*rom this project's earliest beginnings, we were constantly buoyed by the enthusiasm of all with whom we discussed our work. For months, we were in almost daily receipt of the help and encouragement of people and institutions from across the nation. Under such circumstances, any attempt at acknowledging some carries with it the risk of neglecting others who deserve our appreciation. Yet we feel compelled to mention those whose names evoke special memories and who are as certainly a part of the unfolding of these stories as we are.

We are able to produce a volume such as this from the splendid isolation of Bozeman, Montana, largely due to the resources available at Montana State University's Renne Library and to the help and cooperation extended by Kathryn Kujawa and Elizabeth Waddington of the interlibrary loan staff of the Bozeman Public Library. The prompt and courteous responses of the staffs of university and municipal libraries, private collections, and state archives across the United States contributed greatly to the success of our research efforts. Some of these institutions are named in these paragraphs, while others are cited in the brief source notes at the end of the book.

We are also indebted to the many individuals who, through private communications, shared their research findings, technical expertise, or personal recollections. For example, throughout our work on Kate Barnard we benefitted from the insightful comments of Julee Short, whose University of Oklahoma thesis was one of the first in-depth biographical studies of Barnard. Many other Oklahomans encouraged us to tell Barnard's story and/or provided us with invaluable resource materials, and for these efforts we offer our thanks to U.S. Senator David Boren; Angie Debo, historian; Linda Edmondson, Muskogee columnist; Joanie Boyne of the *Daily Oklahoman*; and Nancy Nunnally of the Oklahoma Department of Corrections.

Ferreting out the details of Williamina Fleming's story was one of our most difficult and frustrating tasks. At the moment of our deepest despair, Barbara Welther of Harvard College Observatory encouraged us to persist and offered fresh insights and further leads. Pamela Mack, now of Worcester Polytechnic Institute, provided her Harvard honors thesis. Dr. Georgeanne Caughlin of Montana State University read and corrected our manuscript, thereby saving us a few technical embarrassments.

Orie Latham Hatcher's story can be told here because much of it was revealed in an unpublished doctoral dissertation. The author of that work, Dr. Belinda Friedman, now of Columbia College, South Carolina, merits our thanks for her support and encouragement throughout the project. Through Ellen Gartrell of Perkins Library, Duke University, we had access to tapes made by Delores Brien of Bryn Mawr. But our greatest gratitude goes to Virginia DeMott Cox, Dr. Hatcher's niece, who, by letters, tapes, and phone calls, patiently shared all her memories and stayed with us until we had the story right.

Mary McDowell's story came alive for us through the invaluable, on-the-spot assistance of Elizabeth Mentzer, who served as our surrogate researcher at the Chicago Historical Society and whose belief in McDowell's worth intensified our own.

Annie Smith Peck's story took on new life because of the interest shown by Laura and Guy Waterman, Caroline Schimmel, and Tom Waldorf, all of whom shared their Peck resources and/or their mountaineering expertise. Materials obtained from the Sophia Smith Collection at Smith College proved invaluable, as did papers held by the American Geographical Society.

We feel most fortunate that in telling the story of Ida Wells-Barnett we had the endorsement and encouragement of her daughter Alfreda M. Duster of Chicago, who read and corrected our manuscript, and of Nathan I. Huggins, Chairman, Afro-American Studies, Harvard University.

If we have captured the spirit of Candace Thurber Wheeler, it is because we were guided throughout our research by the personal insights offered by her great-niece, Caroline Pullman, who generously shared family memories, letters, and photographs. Madeleine Stern's *We the Women* gave us our first in-depth view of Candace Wheeler, and the author herself offered enthusiastic support. The Stowe-Day Foundation was a constant and reliable resource.

We also extend our gratitude to the friends and professionals close to home who read our drafts and asked significant questions: Dr. Saku Srinanthakumar, Gwen Peterson, Jean Rhodes, Angie B. Smith, and Fleda B. Peavy.

Finally, we wish to give special thanks to David Toberisky, an unflappable editor, without whom, of course, this project would not have come to print.

~ *Sara Josephine Baker* ~
Questioning the Unquestionable

*S*he was probably too late. Dr. Baker knew it from the way the
old woman shook her head as she asked her which floor the
O'Conners lived on. Standing on the dimly lit landing, she steeled
herself against what might be waiting in the room beyond. The door
swung open almost at once, and in the yellow light of the dingy oil
lamp she saw a tiny wisp of a girl, barefoot and wearing only a
ragged, sun-faded smock. Still clinging to the doorknob, the hollow-
eyed child stared up without a word, looking as if she were ready at
any moment to disappear into the darkness.

"I'm here to see the baby."

The child opened the door a bit wider and nodded in the direction of a woman lying on a mattress in the room's darkest corner. A
toddler lay sleeping at her feet. In a dirty cotton blanket next to his
mother lay the newborn.

Dr. Baker knelt in the litter that surrounded the bed. Calling for the lamp, she placed it so that its light fell upon the infant. Limp, scrawny legs protruded from foul-smelling, badly soiled diapers. Uncontrolled diarrhea and severe dehydration, with summer just begun. This small life was about to become another statistic.

As Dr. Baker finished her examination, the baby's mother wearily brushed a fly from the milk-encrusted nipple of a bottle that lay half-hidden in the ragged bedding.

"See there," she said, holding the bottle up to the lamp, "he couldn't even get down half of it. Hadn't the strength." Then staring blankly into the darkness, she added flatly, "He'll be with the saints before morning, won't he, Doctor?"

Looking from the haunted eyes of the tired mother to the listless form within the blanket's threadbare folds, Sara Josephine Baker was swept by a sense of helplessness. Within the crowded tenements of New York City there were 1,500 other babies who would not last the week, 1,500 other mothers who, before the week was out, would follow small white caskets to tiny graves.

Years later Dr. Baker recalled how that fiery summer of 1902 relentlessly claimed its victims. Among the immigrant families, the suffocating heat turned the "melting pot of Manhattan Island . . . [into] a germ culture." Milk soured, bacteria multiplied, flies and cockroaches spread deadly filth. "You could hardly go a block without meeting a little white funeral," she wrote, and overwhelmed by this "great waste," she made a decision. "My problem," she wrote, "was how to prevent it." Over the next 20 years, Dr. Baker's solution to that problem was to save the lives of over 10,000 babies.

Examining dying babies in insect-ridden tenement houses in the Hell's Kitchen area of New York City had not been a part of the childhood plans of Sara Josephine Baker. Born in 1873, daughter of a well-to-do lawyer, she grew up in Poughkeepsie, New York, a child surrounded by the niceties of life and filled with vague, pleasant dreams of someday attending nearby Vassar. Her mother, Jenny Brown Baker, had been one of the first to enter Matthew Vassar's new college for young women, and her contacts there brought a steady stream of Vassar students and teachers into the Baker family's spacious home.

Orlando Daniel Moser Baker, a self-made, self-educated man, was as studied and disciplined as his name implied. Never speaking an unnecessary word, he was a constant example of economy of energy and resources, a virtue exemplified by his practice of buying 7 identical pairs of shoes at once and wearing each pair only one day of the week in order to get maximum use from them. Even when he played, this kindly Quaker did so with deliberation. For his pursuit of woodworking, he accumulated enough equipment to meet the needs of most professional carpenters, and the quality of his work rivaled theirs. As a fisherman he could compete with the region's best anglers, and he owned enough fishing lures and rods to stock a sporting goods store.

From babyhood, little Josephine followed her father about, having early resolved to "make it up to [him] for having been born a girl." As a third daughter, she heard reports of his disappointment at her birth, and she spent her early years trying to be as good as any boy her father might have had. Those efforts did not flag even when, at age 3, Josephine welcomed a baby brother into the family. Instead, she taught young Robert all the skills she'd learned from her father, and together they ice-boated, fished, and rowed in the Hudson River and romped and played with an otherwise all-boy gang.

Still, she did spend enough time with her mother to become "thoroughly trained in the business of being a woman," by which she meant that she was capable of cooking and sewing as well as most any other young woman of her time. Exposed as often to what others termed "tomboy" activities as to activities that would have been labeled thoroughly "feminine" pursuits, she chose what she enjoyed from both worlds, never feeling obligated to conform to one way of life or another.

An important influence in young Josephine's life was a Quaker aunt who had already lived nearly a century by the time Josephine was old enough to remember her. It was Aunt Abby who gave her her "first acquaintance with skepticism and non-conformity." Simply for the sake of being different, Aunt Abby deliberately turned night into day, a secret only the children knew, since the grown-ups never bothered to notice the strange pattern of her sleeping and waking hours. And they never bothered to stay around when the sweet old lady read Bible stories to her nieces and nephews, either. Thus they never knew that every story ended with Aunt Abby's quietly reminding the children that these were obviously very silly stories with not a word of truth to them and that they were never to believe such tales.

Though they continued to go to Sunday School, Dr. Baker later recalled that "it was hardly possible for us to take much stock in Jonah and the whale from that time on." It was Aunt Abby who taught her one of life's most valuable lessons—"it [is] possible to question the unquestionable." Apparently, Aunt Abby's Bible stories were the beginning of what Dr. Baker later termed her "desire to question the right and wrong of all accepted doctrines."

Her early schooling encouraged such questioning. She was enrolled at Miss Thomas's, a school for girls founded by 2 spinster sisters and housed in an old home on Poughkeepsie's Academy Street. At Miss Thomas's, there were no graded classes, no examinations, no report cards, and no graduation exercises. The 3 to 4 girls in each study group progressed according to their ability to master the subjects being taught, and Josephine Baker moved along well, always looking vaguely ahead to her years at Vassar.

Then, shortly after her sixteenth birthday, her world abruptly changed. Her brother died, and 3 months later, her father also, victims of a typhoid epidemic that swept through Poughkeepsie. Shattered by this double tragedy, she later recalled that they had been "an understanding trio," and when the 2 died so close together "there seemed very little left to live for."

Young Josephine's dream of Vassar suddenly faded. She felt her primary responsibility was to earn enough money to support her mother and surviving sister, and she cast about for a way in which she could make a living while doing something she would find challenging and worthwhile. Perhaps because of her recent experience with a kindly doctor who helped her through a severe knee injury, perhaps because of her need to help those less fortunate than she, perhaps because it was the only profession she could easily enter without first earning a college degree, Josephine decided to become a doctor. Taking $5,000, all the money that could be spared, she set out for New York City. To Josephine, the idea of becoming a doctor seemed quite practical. To her relatives, even to her mother at first, it seemed totally preposterous, "an unheard of . . . harebrained and unwomanly scheme."

Once in New York, she learned that while Vassar would have honored the no-diploma education she had received from the two sisters in Poughkeepsie, the New York Women's Medical College would not. Her only hope of being admitted was to go back home and study to pass the New York Regents Exams. Her determination carried her through a year of intensive study, during which time she taught herself chemistry and biology, subjects beyond the scope of Miss Thomas's school.

Once she was back and settled in New York City, she had still more call for courage and determination. Josephine Baker's first year at the Women's Medical College was so hard and so lonely that only thoughts of the skeptical relatives at home kept her from giving up. Her years of medical school were later described as "four long years of grinding study, four years of irresponsible happiness, and four years so remote from the real work of the world that one might as well have been in a convent." In spring of 1898, Sara Josephine Baker graduated second in a class of 18.

She was offered an opportunity to intern at the New England Hospital for Women and Children in Boston, and she took it gladly, for there was, at that time, no chance of a woman's getting into a large general hospital. Three months of her internship were spent in the outpatient department in a clinic in Fayette Street, a clinic serving the city's worst slum areas. Her work there taught her that "luridly colored pictures in ponderous medical texts meant actual fever and pain and delirium and mutilation, and that those crisp summaries of what to do about this or that physical ailment . . . were of distressingly little help to an inexperienced beginner."

She shared these valuable lessons with her roommate and fellow intern, Dr. Florence Laighton. Later the two friends took an apartment in New York City near the western border of Central Park and set up practice there. Dr. Baker's first year's proceeds totaled $185, and her friend's income was little better. It was evident that their family practice was growing, yet not fast enough to keep them solvent. On impulse, Dr. Baker answered an advertisement for a civil service position and secured an appointment as medical inspector for New York City's Department of Public Health. The salary was only $30 a month, but that amount was nearly double what she'd earned in her first year of private practice.

Dr. Baker was responsible for making calls on the classrooms of the city schools to determine the number of sick children, the nature of their illnesses, and the likelihood of contagion. It was dismal, discouraging work, for inspecting school children was a hopeless task, one that her fellow inspectors didn't even bother to do. She felt guilty—not because she shirked her assigned duties, but because she felt that the work she did accomplished so little. She stuck the job out, despite its frustrations, for she badly needed the dollar a day she received for giving an hour a day to this task.

Then, in 1902, under a new commissioner of public health, changes were made that opened the door to what was to be her life's work. The incoming assistant sanitary supervisor, Dr. Walter Benzel, offered her the newly created job of seeking out sick babies for the department—at $100 per month. For 6 hours each day she "climbed stair after stair, knocked on door after door, met drunk after drunk, filthy mother after filthy mother, and dying baby after dying baby."

The work was even more discouraging and depressing than her work as school inspector. She was assigned the Hell's Kitchen area of the city, an area populated by Irish immigrants and blacks, an area where infants were born with odds so heavily weighted against them that they were usually doomed before Dr. Baker was able to find them. During that first summer of her assignment, an average of 1,500 babies died each week in New York City, most of them "lean, miserable, wailing souls carried off wholesale by dysentery."

She was hardly sentimental about the sufferings she observed, later recalling that she "had a sincere conviction that [the babies] would all be better off dead than so degradingly alive." Yet, because she sensed in the hapless infants "an instinct for life," she pressed on in her attempts to help.

They were hard to help. Parents were glad enough to have the doctor come when their babies grew seriously ill, but they showed little interest in her directives aimed at preventing illness. In general, the mothers were depressingly fatalistic—babies always died in the summer and there was no point in trying to change that.

Unfortunately, many of Dr. Baker's medical colleagues seemed equally fatalistic. They were convinced that long, hot summers in crowded tenements would continue to take their toll on the infant population of New York City. One fellow medical inspector severely upbraided Dr. Baker, calling her "thoroughly unethical" because she actually bothered to look for hopelessly sick babies and report them, warning her that she was risking the anger of her colleagues because her reports made them look inefficient.

The young man was right. Soon Dr. Benzel, well aware of the work habits of his staff members, dropped several of the negligent inspectors and made Dr. Josephine Baker his office assistant. From that time she was moved to various jobs within the department, usually as a troubleshooter who found solutions to problems others hadn't managed to solve. She invaded the lodging houses of the Bowery to inoculate sleeping drunks against smallpox, became the department's expert on cerebrospinal meningitis while fighting an epidemic, was put in charge of noise and nuisance inspections, wrote pamphlets on rabies and sunstroke, inspected swimming pools, became the first editor of the Health Department's new monthly bulletin for the medical profession, served as sanitary inspector of schools and other public places, and was assigned the formidable task of tracking down "Typhoid Mary" Malone.

Then in 1907 the Bureau of Municipal Research asked Dr. Baker's help in investigating the reasons behind New York City's high death rate. A preliminary study showed her that one-third of those who died each year were under 5 years of age and one-fifth were under one year of age. The scenes of Hell's Kitchen came quickly to mind. If it was already too late to help sick babies by the time doctors had sought them out, the department would have to start sooner—they would have to find ways of keeping the babies from falling ill in the first place.

Authorities were not easily convinced. There weren't enough doctors and nurses to help those who were sick. Why waste the time of the medical staff on those who were well?

But Dr. Baker persisted. Cutting the death rate depended more upon keeping well babies well than on trying to bring sick babies back to health. A dozen years earlier she herself hadn't been very concerned with well children either. She had flunked "The Normal Child" in medical school, the only course she had ever failed, and she failed it out of sheer boredom. Forced to take the course over and angry with herself for not passing it the first time, she resolved to learn all she could about "that little pest, the normal child." It was that knowledge that served as the basis for all she was now to do in the field of preventive child hygiene.

In 1908 the Bureau of Municipal Research recommended that the New York City Department of Health establish a division for preventive tactics, a division with Dr. Baker as its chief. No staff, no money were promised, just a title and an idea. Aware of how hard it would be to convince city officials to spend money on well people, Dr. Baker knew she had to prove that her plan would work before she could hope to gain funds to carry it out.

Her instinct for thrift and maximum use of available resources, instilled by her father's example, served her well. She realized that she had a huge, well-trained staff available over the summer months, if only the city could be persuaded to let her use them. When the schools closed each June, the city's corps of 30 school nurses were off duty. And June marked the start of the diarrhea season, which inevitably swept off thousands of babies. With the health department's permission, school nurses were assigned to Dr. Baker for what was to be a landmark experiment in preventive child hygiene.

Dr. Baker picked her research subjects with great care. In her earlier work she had learned much about the people who populated the various districts of the city. Now she chose to concentrate her efforts in the Lower East Side, a section largely populated by recently landed Italians. She knew that since the East Side had one of the highest infant death rates in the city, the neighborhood should offer ample opportunity for drastic, easily observed improvements. Furthermore, she had learned that the family-centered, open-minded Italians seemed more eager to learn American ways than did other immigrant groups she had worked with. The Lower East Side seemed the ideal place for trying out her theories.

Because the city required that all births be recorded, Dr. Baker and her nurses had daily reports of the arrival of new infants in their area. Accordingly, a nurse was sent to visit the mother and the newborn and to give detailed instructions for keeping the baby well. Invariably, the nurse advised breastfeeding as the safest, surest method of nourishing the child; discussed the importance of sufficient ventilation, especially through the summer months; urged frequent bathing; discussed proper summer clothing; and recommended a daily airing in the little strip of park around the corner. These instructions are considered basic principles of hygiene today, but they were relatively new concepts then, especially to those immigrant mothers. Though skeptical at first, the mothers became enthusiastic when they saw that their summer newborns were not only surviving but thriving, despite temperatures that soared to record highs.

When the experiment was completed, statistics showed 1,200 fewer deaths in that corner of the East Side than there had been the summer before, while all the other areas of the city had had as many deaths as ever. Dr. Baker's preventive techniques were credited with the reduced rate, and health authorities and grateful families finally accepted the fact that summer heat need not kill babies. Dr. Baker later remarked, "There, if we have to be dramatic about it, was the actual beginning of my life work."

On August 19, 1908, the Department of Public Health officially created the Division of Child Hygiene and made 35-year-old Sara Josephine Baker its chief. This was the world's first government bureau concerned with child hygiene, and Dr. Baker was the first woman in the United States to be appointed to an administrative or executive position within a department of health. Also the first person to act on the idea that preventive medicine was a function of government, she led her agency to implement ideas that would drastically change the concept of pediatric health care for the entire nation and, indeed, for much of the world.

Money came in fairly generous amounts, once the effectiveness of the program had been demonstrated. But the dramatic experiment that proved the effectiveness of preventive care was only a beginning. That summer of 1908 the infant mortality rate for New York City was 144 per 1,000 births, even with the 1,200 babies saved in the Lower East Side. While that was considerably better than the 160 per 1,000 recorded the summer before, there was obviously still more work to be done if infant mortality rates were to be lowered for the entire city.

But saving babies wasn't Dr. Baker's only work. She was increasingly busy with the private practice she and Dr. Laighton shared, and her Division of Child Hygiene was commissioned to do many tasks that had formerly fallen to other divisions within the Department of Health. Far from being intimidated by so much responsibility, Dr. Baker embraced her work. From her earliest childhood, she had been challenged, not cowed, by seemingly impossible tasks and inspired, not daunted, by cries of skeptics. Because of her father's example, she was able to utilize time and resources effectively, and because of her Aunt Abby's skepticism, she felt no qualms about challenging accepted methods of doing things, even when those methods happened to be the ones she herself had established.

In 1909, when seeking out well babies over the entire city failed to improve the infant mortality rate much beyond the rate of improvement shown for 1908, Dr. Baker decided that the summer program alone was not enough, and she looked for other methods of attacking the problem. By 1911, she had designed another solution, a "milk station" program. Nurses in 15 milk stations in various parts of the city took a brief history of each baby brought in, dispensed high-quality milk at lower-than-market prices, gave out instructions for using that milk in a simple, easy-to-use formula devised by Dr. Baker and a committee of pediatricians, and gave the baby an appointment for a medical checkup.

The stations made no attempt to treat sick babies but referred them to private or health department doctors. The milk station program was highly successful; it was estimated that the 15 milk stations saved over 1,000 lives in 1911. By 1912, 40 more milk stations were opened, with 55 in operation by the close of that year.

Some doctors criticized Dr. Baker for calling the centers "milk stations," saying that such a name might cause some mothers to assume that their breast milk was inferior to the cow's-milk formula dispensed at the stations. In response to such critics, Dr. Baker displayed one of her greatest strengths—the ability to separate the ideal from the real. A staunch advocate of breastfeeding, she maintained that "if every mother nursed her baby [there would be] but a small problem . . . [but] as things are, in modern city and industrial life, this is out of the question." Under such circumstances thousands of babies owed their lives to the cow's-milk formula dispensed at Dr. Baker's stations.

This same practical philosophy was evident in the way she handled what most physicians considered to be one of the city's most obvious causes of infant mortality—the work of untrained midwives. By the early twentieth century the practice of midwifery was becoming less and less common across the United States, but in New York City, where immigrant families followed the ways of the old country, midwives rather than physicians were often in attendance at deliveries. Properly trained, midwives could be an asset; ill-trained, they were a definite threat to the lives and health of mothers as well as infants. Often midwives were ignorant, superstitious, and motivated only by money. Many performed illegal abortions to increase their income.

In 1910 official estimates put the number of midwives practicing in New York City at 1,850; it was thought that they accounted for 45 percent of the city's recorded births. Dr. Baker suspected that there might be as many as 4,000 midwives practicing in the city. She decided to begin her attack on the problems caused by the unscrupulous or untrained midwife by requiring all midwives to obtain a license in order to continue their practice. Qualifications were simple enough—attendance at 20 or more deliveries performed by a doctor allowed one to earn the certificate.

In order to push for still better training, Dr. Baker set up a midwives' school of obstetrics at Bellevue Hospital, eventually refusing to license any midwives who weren't graduates of this school or of a European school of equal standing. The course was free, took 6 months, and turned out well-trained women.

Despite the obvious success of her program for training and licensing midwives, Dr. Baker faced the continued opposition of those doctors who saw a physician-attended delivery at a hospital as the only safe method of birthing. In reply to these claims, Dr. Baker presented statistics that showed higher incidence of infection in hospital deliveries than in home deliveries. Doctors who attempted to disprove her statements and her figures only succeeded in unearthing statistics showing that the rate of hospital-induced infection for mothers and babies was even worse than Dr. Baker had declared it to be. Again, she had successfully questioned the unquestionable.

That same attitude was evident in her response to an appeal to outlaw a practice brought to public attention by John Spargo's *The Bitter Cry of the Children*. Spargo's bestseller decried the number of infant deaths caused by the "little mother" system, a widespread practice of leaving young, inexperienced girls in full charge of their baby brothers and sisters. In the years that followed, Spargo and others pressured those in authority to outlaw this potentially dangerous system. In characteristic fashion, Dr. Baker met the challenge of these crusaders by first recognizing that, given the conditions that forced both parents into employment and provided no adequate day care, the "little mother" system was a reality of life in some sections of New York City. Realizing that her bureau "could not afford the luxury of saying things should or should not be . . . [but] had to work realistically with the raw materials and situations at hand," Dr. Baker devised a very practical solution to the problem.

If the "little mother" system was a necessity, then it was the bureau's job to train young girls to do their jobs well. Dr. Baker first approached the New York City school board with the idea of a course in child care. When they called the idea preposterous, she asked her friend, Margaret Knox, principal of Public School 15, to sponsor the city's first Little Mothers' League. Soon nurses were instructing young students at Public School 15 in all aspects of baby care—from feeding to exercising and dressing.

Excited by what they learned, the girls not only pressed all their new-found knowledge into service in their own homes but also canvassed their neighborhoods, urging mothers to bring their infants to baby health stations. Soon Little Mothers' Leagues were flourishing in other schools in New York City, across the nation, and even abroad.

But the successful training of midwives and of "little mothers" did not reduce infant mortality rates enough to satisfy Dr. Baker. As she continued to study carefully gathered statistics, she noted that the highest death rates were occurring not among slum babies in tenement rows, but among foundlings in some of the city's best-run hospital nurseries. Although care, food, and hygiene in the hospitals noted was of unquestioned excellence, 50 percent of the orphaned babies were dying. High death rates among these babies seemed as puzzling as the unusually high death rates found among babies of the city's wealthiest families.

Dr. Baker now declared that what the foundlings lacked was attention, "old-fashioned, sentimental mothering, the kind that psychologists deny." The announcement was astounding to physicians and psychologists alike. The first group had maintained that good food, good hygiene, and good care were enough, and the second group was, at that time, warning mothers against the dangers of too much pampering.

Ignoring their objections, Dr. Baker announced what seemed a totally outrageous plan: In order to save the foundlings, she would take them out of their sterile, carefully monitored environment, where well-trained nurses met their physical needs, and place them in homes of New York's slum districts in order that "maternally minded women" could meet their needs to be loved as well as their needs to be changed, bathed, and fed. For their efforts, these foster families would receive $10 a month, with those who took on cases considered nearly hopeless receiving an extra $5.

In January of 1913, the *New York Times* announced the results of this daring experiment. The 2,844 foundlings boarded out fared far better than those left in the sterile confines of the orphans' hospitals. The death rate for these foster babies was one in 3, as opposed to one in 2 for the institutionalized infants. Improvements in premature infants were even more dramatic, as half of the premature babies boarded out prospered, while all of those left in institutions died.

Encouraged by her success in reducing the mortality rate of orphaned infants, Dr. Baker drew what seemed an important parallel between the high death rates of institutionalized babies and those of babies from the city's wealthiest families. She surmised that the care of the baby born into a rich family was similar to that of the foundling housed in an institution—a nurse or nanny gave the infant "the best of care with all the impersonal efficiency of a well-intentioned machine." Like the orphans, these babies received little loving attention, and it was Dr. Baker's firm conviction that

> many a baby has died for lack of . . . that sense of being at home in a new world which only fond personal attention from his mother or the psychological equivalent can give him. He needs it even more than he needs butterfat and fresh diapers. . . . he needs the personal equation to give him a reason for living.

Despite her insights into the problem, Dr. Baker was never able to achieve the dramatic reduction in infant mortality among the wealthy that she had achieved among the poor, possibly because wealthy parents saw very little connection between what a public health doctor did with tenement babies and orphans and what responsible, well-educated parents did with their own well-scrubbed, well-dressed little charges.

Certainly the wealthy knew of her work, for her consuming interest in the health and well-being of the city's infants, her infectious enthusiasm, and her boundless energy did not go unpublicized. In January of 1913, the *New York Times* called her drastic reduction in infant mortality rates "the most remarkable feature of the city's record health year."

Dr. Baker had reduced the death rate among the city's babies by more than one-third, but she was still far from satisfied. Sure that even more lives could be saved, she studied the statistics of the bureau's 5-year records, 1907 to 1912, seeking clues to saving still more lives. The figures told her that the most striking improvements in infant mortality rates had come through preventing deaths due to intestinal, respiratory, and contagious diseases, diseases upon which most of her efforts had been centered. There had been no significant reduction in deaths occurring during or shortly after childbirth, specifically, those deaths due to weakness or ill health of the mother.

Prompted by this statistical clue, Dr. Baker now gave increased attention to the area of prenatal care. She maintained that mothers-to-be who were victims of tuberculosis and other serious diseases or who were alcoholic, poorly nourished, or overworked were likely to die themselves or to deliver weak and unhealthy babies.

But this time Dr. Baker was too far ahead of her time to be taken seriously. In 1913 her statements on the importance of pre-natal care were largely ignored, despite the fact that she maintained she could do little more to lower infant mortality rates until problems in prenatal care were solved. As late as 1927, she was still advocating these improvements, telling the obstetrics section of the American Medical Association that mothers as well as babies were dying due to lack of proper prenatal care and to inefficient, unsafe obstetrical practices.

In a presentation later published in the *AMA Journal*, she up-braided her fellow physicians for their part in allowing a maternal death rate higher than that of any other civilized country in the world except Chile. She called upon doctors to use the knowledge and resources available to them to improve this dismal record and thereby save the lives of thousands of mothers and babies.

All the while Dr. Baker was involved in saving babies, the work for which she received greatest recognition, she was simultaneously supervising other programs in preventive child hygiene. Her success in carrying out all of these programs at once stemmed, in part, from her insistence that she and her staff should devote their time to the real problems at hand rather than to bureaucratic paper shuffling. To make this ideal possible, without jeopardizing the accumulation of the vital statistics so essential to her work, she designed a record-keeping system that was so streamlined and efficient that it was soon adopted by health departments across the country.

She streamlined school inspections as well, redesigning the form of the examination so that it was more easily conducted and gave better, more reliable results. Under her guidance, the incidence of such skin diseases as scabies, ringworm, and impetigo was drastically reduced, as were cases of trachoma, a highly infectious and potentially blinding eye disease.

In the course of her practice, Dr. Baker conducted a thorough investigation into the incidence and treatment of a very common school-age problem—tonsil and adenoid infections. Seeing a need for a simplified method of surgery but unable to gain the cooperation of the city's regular hospitals, she opened 6 small clinics where surgical procedures were limited exclusively to adenoidectomies and tonsilectomies. In a practice that is now commonplace, the children were hospitalized the night before surgery and informed of what would happen to them—including use of anesthetic—and why.

Following surgery the next morning, they were observed for several hours, fed ice cream, doted upon, and released. In 6 years, thousands of these operations were performed in Dr. Baker's special clinics, all without a single fatality, a single septic sore throat, or a single postoperative hemorrhage. When the general hospitals became convinced of the wisdom of Dr. Baker's methods, they incorporated them as standard procedure, and the special hospitals were closed.

Because she sensed that the most effective method of health care for children was the education of parents, that effort became a major thrust of her work in school health. Under Dr. Baker's guidance, Dr. Lina Rogers, one of the first public health school nurses in the nation, developed a staff of nurses who instructed parents in de-licing their children, in dressing skin diseases, and in preventing and treating trachoma. In 1915 there were thousands of cases of diseases such as these in the public schools; by 1930 there were only 2 or 3 cases in all the city's schools.

Dr. Baker's assaults on health problems of school-aged children were not all unqualified successes. Her campaign for the prevention of tooth decay might even be classified as a failure, though through no fault of her own. Faced with the lack of interest in parents who showed little concern with their youngster's rotten or prematurely lost baby teeth, she worked to teach students the proper care of their teeth. She imported all the graduates of the nation's first school of dental hygiene and had them conduct toothbrush drills in the school, but to no avail. The children's dental records showed no significant improvement, and Dr. Baker was forced to admit that well-scrubbed teeth still decayed. Not one to waste energy in an area that showed no gains, she conceded defeat, her campaign victimized by too-limited knowledge of the causes of dental caries. She had had the right idea—tooth decay could be prevented—but this time she was touching on preventive dentistry, a field that was not firmly established until long after her death.

She met defeat in still another area—that of proper classroom ventilation—although here she was able to show indisputable evidence that her theories of prevention were sound. Her research for work toward a doctorate in public health, the first such degree to be won by a woman, proved conclusively that well-ventilated classrooms meant fewer incidents of upper respiratory disease. Though her findings were published in the *American Journal of Public Health*, schools continued to maintain tomb-like atmospheres. Students were deprived of adequate fresh air for the sake of keeping down school heat bills and keeping out distracting noises.

Though she could not keep school windows open, she did keep the schools themselves open when the influenza epidemic of 1918 swept the nation, causing health departments of other large cities to close the schools. Dr. Baker, again daring to question accepted practices, convinced her superiors to hold New York City schools open on the grounds that, properly monitored, they were the safest places for children to be. Despite a severe public outcry, New York stood firm as the only major city whose schools ran as usual through the epidemic. When the flu outbreak was declared officially over, statistics revealed that the city's 6- to 15-year-olds were the only age group that had experienced no epidemic pattern.

In other areas touching on child health, Dr. Baker was equally willing to challenge accepted opinions. She spoke out against the rush to embrace the new field of child psychology, reminding parents that children have always been "naughty" and that they have always been easily and effectively corrected by various old-fashioned methods, since "ordinary badness" had never before been considered "a pathological condition." She noted that "Nowadays if a child is anything but a little robot he is taken to a child psychologist to have the cause discovered. The net result is that mothers are unduly apprehensive and children are watched so closely that the tension is disastrous for both. . . ."

She could state such views, controversial as they were, and still maintain her popularity, for her record spoke for itself. In the early summer of 1908 she had begun her work as chief of the Division of Child Hygiene with no staff and no money. By 1913, with a staff of nearly 500 and a budget of over $600,000, her division was the largest in the New York Department of Public Health. And it was also one of the most effective. New York City's infant mortality rate was, at that point, the lowest of all major cities in the world. Within the United States, one of every 5 babies died before the age of one year, while in New York City, only one of 12 died during the first year of life.

When interviewed in 1913 concerning this admirable record, Dr. Baker made it clear that her main concerns at that time were to continue to work for improvement in health standards in New York City and to share with other public health officials the methods used to reduce infant mortality. She had been instrumental in the establishment of a federal Children's Bureau in 1912, and she had set as her goal the creation of a Division of Child Hygiene in every state health department in the nation. She planned to retire as chief of the New York City Division of Child Hygiene when that goal was accomplished.

She talked freely and openly about these and other plans with the city's newspaper reporters, for she had recognized from her first days on the job how powerful an ally a newspaper was. She had learned early on how to use publicity to interest the public in her projects, and during the war years she put those skills to particularly good use. Telling reporters that "It's six times safer to be a soldier in the trenches of France than to be born a baby in the United States," she invited headlines that would ensure support of her programs.

Generally, Dr. Baker had found that being the only woman executive in the Department of Public Health meant her work received more than its share of publicity. Being a woman also gave her an inside track with Tammany Hall politicians, since their "natural Irish politeness" made them reluctant ever to give her a flat refusal. But being a woman had its liabilities, too. Men who had had no difficulty in working *with* her in her early days with the department presented their resignations when they learned they would be working *for* her in the newly formed Division of Child Hygiene. To offset this reaction, she suggested a one-month trial period, during which time she subtly managed to give each of these men some small title or position of responsibility within the division. To a man, they decided to remain under her authority at the end of the probationary period.

Being a woman caused her other problems as well. Her most minor mistakes received more attention than did the major errors of men in similar positions of responsibility. Thus, though she was glad the press saw her gender as reason for giving her work valuable publicity, within the health department she tried to de-emphasize her femininity. She adopted a style of dress that she felt made her presence less obtrusive, wearing man-tailored suits, shirtwaists, stiff collars, and four-in-hand ties because "the last thing [she] wanted was to be conspicuously feminine when working with men." Though she acknowledged that these suits were "a trifle expensive," she felt that "they more than paid their way as buffers."

In her tailored suits, Dr. Josephine Baker moved freely and easily in her predominantly male world, determined to do her job well, to make absolutely certain that her work was "a success and equal to the best that might be done by a man in that man-made world."

In her later years she was drawn into the women's suffrage movement almost by "psychological suction." When she realized that intelligent, well-educated women were being denied the vote while semiliterate men exercised that privilege, she joined 4 or 5 other women in founding the College Equal Suffrage League. Wearing academic caps and gowns, the women in her group were among the 500 who, in 1915, marched in the first annual Fifth Avenue Suffrage Parade. Dr. Baker made speeches for women's suffrage and was present in the Oval Office when President Wilson announced that he supported the suffrage movement and gave its leaders permission to use his support to help their cause.

In later life, Dr. Baker realized that the power of the vote was not enough. She felt that women should have maintained a solid bloc, even after obtaining the vote, since only by political solidarity could they ever hope to achieve effective change. By 1939, obvious inequalities in job opportunities led her to the disappointing realization that, despite the vote, women had actually lost ground in some areas. The federal Child Welfare Program, initially organized under 3 male and 45 female state directors, was, by 1939, administered by 36 male and 12 female directors. Dr. Baker was grudgingly aware that her dreams for women's rights had not become realities.

She was disappointed in other areas, too. As a member of the Heterodoxy Club, a group of woman "pacifists and radicals" active even before the First World War, she worked for peace, yet she lived to see her country involved in two global conflicts. And though she was "enough of a socialist" to want a minimum liveable wage for all, she saw at close range the continued sufferings of the poor.

She was not able to end poverty, but her own courageous, innovative work gave the children of the poor a chance for fuller, happier lives. In her efforts to share her ideas, she delivered lectures before members of the medical profession and wrote more than 50 articles for professional medical and health journals. Her work and her discussions of that work had a significant impact on the American public, and by 1923 there were agencies for preventive child hygiene operating in every state and in several foreign countries.

She had attained the goal she had proclaimed publicly as the capstone of her career, and in 1923 she retired from her position as chief of the Bureau of Child Hygiene. In that year, the infant mortality rate for New York City was one-third the rate it had been when she began her tenure, and cities around the country were beginning to show similar improvements.

At age 50, she was hardly ready to retire from active duty, but she was ready to serve in new ways. From 1922 to 1924 she represented the United States on the Health Committee of the League of Nations, the first woman of professional rank to hold such a position. In 1923 she was appointed consulting director in maternity and child hygiene of the U.S. Children's Bureau. In her retirement years she served on over 25 such committees for children's health, and she served one term as president of the American Medical Women's Association.

Those later years of her life were primarily devoted to making her ideas on child hygiene known outside the New York City area. In 2 decades she wrote over 200 articles for popular magazines such as *Ladies Home Journal* and *Parents*, and she wrote 5 books on child and maternal hygiene. She traveled all over the United States and most of Europe delivering lectures to health-care groups, women's clubs, and community organizations. In 1939 she published *Fighting for Life*, an autobiography describing the work of her lifetime. Five years later, in February of 1945, at 72 years of age, her death by cancer ended a life that had made a difference.

Sara Josephine Baker's life's work had laid the foundation for preventive health measures that saved hundreds of thousands of babies. In 1907, the year Dr. Baker became head of the Bureau of Child Hygiene, one out of 6 babies in New York City died before its first birthday. By 1943, largely because Dr. Baker's methods had become widely known and practiced, only one in 20 died during the first year of life. In the early 1980s, one in 100 newborns fails to reach age one, a vastly different picture from that Dr. Baker witnessed when the fiery summers of New York City routinely claimed the lives of 1,500 infants a week.

As the one person most directly responsible for these dramatic changes, Dr. Sara Josephine Baker might well enjoy a look at today's infant mortality statistics. But given her eye for improvement, she would probably be looking beyond the obvious, scanning the statistical breakdowns, seeking for the slightest clue that might help her understand why babies were still dying. Such was her compulsion to save those who are doomed to die before they have really begun to live.

~ *Kate Barnard* ~
Friend of the Friendless

*H*er skirts billowing in the cold, steady wind, Kate Barnard shaded her eyes and peered across a drying cornfield into a rapidly sinking Oklahoma sun. A weathered, nearly barkless cottonwood met her gaze, its bare branches stretched gaunt and gray against the blazing sunset.

"In that tree?" she asked in disbelief. "There couldn't be room enough."

"It's pretty big up close," the ruddy-faced farm woman answered, "and the side toward the river's hollow. Besides," she added with a sharp glance at her two hearers, "elf children don't need room." With that, the woman turned toward the farmhouse from which she had just come.

"Aren't you coming with us?" the man called after her.

"Got work to do," the woman answered without looking around.

As Hobart Huson turned back to the field, he saw Kate Barnard daintily lift her blue skirts enough to clear the weeds that lined the shallow roadway ditch, then move into the field and toward the lone tree that loomed, specter-like, some 75 yards away. Without further hesitation, Huson hurried after her, his collar pulled up against the harshness of the brisk autumn wind.

Breathless, they broke into the open at the same time to stand on the sandy riverbank, only a few yards from the gigantic tree. "I don't see any—" Huson began.

"Hush!" Barnard ordered, pointing to a pile of well-gnawed chicken bones at the tree's base. As if dreading what she might find, she moved slowly to the tree's far side.

There, in the cold, October twilight, she saw 3 half-naked Indian children huddled in a cave-like hollow at the foot of the old tree. As their dark, solemn eyes met her own, they drew even farther into the shelter of the tree. Dropping to her knees on the sandy riverbank, Barnard spoke softly, "Please come out. We won't hurt you."

As she extended an open hand into the hollow, the trapped-animal look in the 3 grimy faces made her suddenly wary of being bitten. Pushing that thought aside, she gently stroked the matted, burr-studded hair of the nearest and smallest child, urging, "Please come. I won't hurt you. I promise. Come."

At her stroking, the tiny child relaxed his hold on his brothers and, as if drawn by some strong if unfamiliar force, melted from the rough hollow of the tree into the smooth hollow of her arms.

The oldest child cried out in alarm, "She's got you now. She knows about the chicken. She's come to take us to jail."

"No, no," she protested, the warmth of her voice melting his fears as she gathered his brother's bare shoulders into the fullness of her shawl. "I've come to take you where you'll never be cold and hungry anymore."

As she rose and handed the toddler to Huson, the oldest boy, as if abruptly deciding to trust her, moved out into the open, half dragging his second brother with him. Sensing his need not to be held, she gave his arm a quick pat. "No," she said, "you'll never be cold and hungry again."

As she and her assistant made their way back to the waiting carriage, the youngest child gathered in Huson's arms, the other 2 following in her wake, Kate Barnard had no way of knowing that her attempts to keep her promise to these 3 children and to hundreds, perhaps thousands, more homeless Indian minors would eventually cost her the political support she needed to continue the work that had gained her the title "The Good Angel of Oklahoma."

Even if she had known that her fight to protect the rights of Indian orphans would end in the destruction of her career and the loss of her own mental and physical health, it is doubtful that this courageous young woman could have turned her back on the evils of a system that destroyed the lives of innocent children.

Having lost her own mother before she was 2, she knew only too well how it felt to be passed from relative to relative, never feeling totally loved and accepted. In later years she reflected that:

> The life of a little boy or girl who has no mother reminds me very much of the winter time when . . . the whole aspect of nature is drear, cold and dismal. . . . Winter is the only synonym of a motherless child['s] life . . . and because I have suffered this winter, I hope to devote my life to such work as will bring a little of the cheer of spring into the darkened lives. . . .

This hope, born of her own dark childhood and expressed in 1907, soon after she began her work as commissioner of Charities and Corrections, was to be realized in the years ahead as Kate Barnard helped move a new state in the direction of compassion and care for the friendless. The loss of her power, her ultimate shattering in the face of mounting personal and political pressures, may also, in some measure, have had its roots in the dark winter of her early years.

Certainly, there was nothing in her birth or early childhood to suggest that by the time she was 30 a newspaper reporter would declare that this "little ninety-six pound bunch of nerves" held more political power in the state of Oklahoma than any man in either party. Born May 23, 1875, just south of Alexandria, Nebraska, she was christened Catherine Ann Barnard. Her mother, Rachel Shiell, a widow with 2 sons by a former marriage, had married John P. Barnard 8 years after the death of her first husband. Of Irish descent, Barnard was a sometime lawyer and surveyor who was a railroad construction worker at the time of his daughter's birth, and by the end of 1875 he'd taken his family to Kirwin, Kansas, anticipating new rail work there.

In January of 1877, Rachel Shiell Barnard and a week-old newborn died, leaving John Barnard with a daughter, 2 stepsons, and 3 city lots. Selling the lots, he paid his wife's bills, then boarded out his stepsons and Kate with their maternal grandparents. Around Kate's sixth birthday, Barnard married again, this time to a woman less than half his age, and Kate went to live with the newlyweds. Two years later, in August of 1883, Anna T. Rose Barnard left him, taking their 2-month-old son Frank with her. For the second time, Kate was left motherless, although she never spoke of this second loss.

Apparently, she spent the next few years in her father's company, although she was, often as not, left to her own supervision. She recalled dreaming of doing "wonderful things, deeds that were good and kind," and she apparently went often to religious services, where she enjoyed plaintive hymns that soothed her soul by reminding her of the eternal presence of "Jesus, Lover of My Soul." Perhaps it was in these early church services that she began to develop the religious conviction that led her to see as ideal a life of self-sacrifice for the benefit of others.

Soon thereafter, John Barnard suffered a great financial loss, which Kate later described as leaving them "thrown into the bottom of the abyss, where the struggle is tooth and nail for bread." Left penniless, John Barnard struck out for Oklahoma's land run of April 22, 1889, when 50,000 men, women, and children raced to stake their claims to unassigned lands being granted to homesteaders. Fourteen-year-old Kate was left behind. Her true feelings at this apparent desertion can only be imagined, but her written memories seem to speak well for Barnard as she notes that she only recalled his shedding tears upon two occasions, once when her mother died and again "when he bade me goodbye and left me with strangers, at the time he entered the terrible 'run' for a free home. . . ."

John Barnard lost the claim he made on that particular run, but he remained in Oklahoma Territory* and was more successful in the 1891 run on Pottawatomie, Sac and Fox, and Iowa lands, claiming a small parcel near Newalla, a community between Shawnee and Oklahoma City.

Barnard then sent for Kate, now age 16, to hold his claim by living on the land while he worked as a lawyer in Oklahoma City. From the frame shanty on a red-clay hill she looked down across scattered blackjack oak and a few straggly cedars to the creek at the bottom. The poor soil supported little more than grass, and Kate, alone with only a black dog for company, held down their claim, did her father's work as postmaster for a nearby village, and lived in relative isolation until 1892. Then, at 18, she moved into Oklahoma City to finish her schooling at St. Joseph's Parochial School and become, around 1896, a schoolteacher.

Soon disillusioned with teaching, she ended that venture around 1902 and attended Oklahoma City Business College for training as a stenographer. From January to mid-March of 1903, armed with her stenographic training, Kate Barnard went to Guthrie, the territorial capital, to serve as assistant to the chief clerk during the seventh Oklahoma Territorial Legislative Assembly. There she got a taste of politics, though she had, as of yet, no inkling that hers was to be a political life. Through her contacts there she was chosen from nearly 500 applicants to serve as secretary and hostess for the Oklahoma Territory's pavilion at the St. Louis World's Fair—The Louisiana Purchase Exposition of 1904.

Turning 29 less than a month after her arrival in St. Louis, the slender, dark-haired little woman of flashing eyes, smooth, high brow, and olive skin, was an attractive representative. She found it

---

* The Territory of Oklahoma, comprising the western half of the present state of Oklahoma, was opened to settlement in the land run of 1889. The eastern half of the present state remained Indian Territory until 1907 when the Twin Territories were joined and Oklahoma became the forty-sixth state.

easy to communicate with the leaders of the exposition, the persons in charge of various booths, and the reporters who flocked to the exhibits. The World's Fair, with its emphasis on industrial and economic progress, was a logical place to talk about social progress as well, and the social work exhibits were Kate Barnard's favorites.

This was the Age of Reform. Muckrakers like Lincoln Steffens, Ida Tarbell, and John Spargo were shocking their readers with graphic accounts of life in the packing plants, the factories, the mines. President Theodore Roosevelt was on his way to a second term, the spirit of reform ran high, and Barnard found herself caught up in the hopes and dreams of various social workers and reformers whose exhibits she described in long letters to the *Daily Oklahoman.*

The people who built and ran exhibits of "model tenements [and] ideal orphans homes" were dreaming great dreams. They would create a better world, ease the suffering of the working class, effect a true democracy. Their enthusiasm fanned the spark that Kate Barnard's own homeless, penniless years had lit. For the first time in her life, she began to have a sense of direction, later calling her months in St. Louis "a milestone in my life leading to higher ideals."

It is likely that her excitement over these lofty ideals was heightened by her growing friendship with Hobart Huson, a correspondent for the *Daily Oklahoman* and also a member of the staff for the Oklahoma exhibit. A man attuned to the plight of the poor, Huson had accumulated a wealth of background information on the major social reformers of the era.

With Huson, Barnard learned social work firsthand, accepting an invitation to work as factory inspector in the slums of St. Louis, then writing newspaper stories that detailed unsafe working conditions and child labor abuses. Later that summer, Barnard spent two months in the Chicago slums, attending Graham Taylor's Chicago School of Civics and Philanthropy. Her work there was financed by the *Daily Oklahoman* in return for a series of articles. Witnessing the horrors of life in the slums, Barnard warned readers at home against letting rapidly growing Oklahoma City develop its own slum districts.

Returning home in late 1904, Barnard moved back into the home she and her father had bought at 205 West Reno. Located in the southern portion of the city, a section that the well-to-do people had left and the poor had invaded, their home was surrounded by crowded houses shared by several families. Though she had been only vaguely aware of these conditions before her stay in St. Louis, she now realized that the West Reno area was fast becoming a bona fide slum district.

Appalled by the hopelessness of her neighbors, she placed a notice asking for donations of clothing and food in an Oklahoma City newspaper. Over 10,000 garments poured in within a relatively short time, and she organized 14 girls into a task force to help her distribute the materials. Soon her home had become unofficial headquarters for the charity effort in Oklahoma City, and she worked tirelessly to provide food, shelter, and medical attention for all people in need.

In less than a year she had aroused the citizens of Oklahoma City to support her efforts to fight the poverty that threatened to destroy men, women, and children who, before her arrival, had been friendless and hopeless. Already these people had learned to look with trust to "Miss Kate" as their provider, and by December of 1905 she had reorganized and become matron of the nearly defunct United Provident Association, a forerunner of today's United Fund.

But Kate Barnard learned quickly not only what charity could do but what it could not do, for despite all her efforts the problems of the poor were not really being solved, and no long-range solutions were in sight. Frustrated, she later called charity "the weakest of weapons with which to combat the problems of poverty, crime, or disease" and declared that "dealing out a biscuit or bun" was not enough. Faced with this truth, she declared that what the people needed was "not charity but justice, and the chance to do an honest day's work for a fair wage." They needed, she said, a "class of legislation, well enforced, which will protect the weaker man against the strong and give him a better opportunity in the battle of life." She then set about to see that they got that opportunity.

Having served in early 1905 as assistant clerk of the Territorial

Legislative Assembly, she had recorded the bills and resolutions passed by both houses and had seen some of the territory's most powerful politicians in action. She saw, as well, the beginning of an alliance between labor unions and the Farmers' Union, an alliance that was to become increasingly powerful in Oklahoma politics.

By late November of 1906, when the Trades and Labor Assembly of Oklahoma established a Woman's Union Label League to create a demand for products bearing union labels, Kate Barnard became the league's first recording secretary. The United Mine Workers, the Railroad Brotherhood, the Farmer's Union, and the Twin Territories Federation of Labor were all fighting for the right she believed was essential if poverty was to be overcome—the right to do an honest day's work for a fair wage. Having seen how pressure groups such as the railroad could lobby for political favors, she began her own efforts to influence local politics, a move she later defended in a letter to a friend and fellow reformer:

> While most of the leaders in the Charity movement deplore the fact that politics should enter our field, I cannot agree with them. I believe that if our people would get out and help elect friends of our measures and defeat our enemies, we should accomplish a great deal more than we can do by getting women's clubs, churches, etc., to pass resolutions and look wise.

Within the city she asked men to vote for candidates who had assured her of their support of charitable efforts, reminding poor workers of the clothes and food she'd provided and explaining that their vote for her candidate would be a returned favor and a means of ensuring that more help would be forthcoming. As founder of Federal Union No. 12374 for the unskilled workers of Oklahoma City's slum district, she led that group in a political effort that helped elect a pro-labor mayor in 1907.

But Kate Barnard's work reached beyond city limits. President Roosevelt's enabling act of June 16, 1906, had empowered Oklahoma's Twin Territories to write a constitution for coming statehood. Now there began a great rush by various interest groups to elect to the constitutional convention delegates who would see that the new document was written to their advantage. Indeed, as Barnard later recalled, "Everything was advocated but the rights of men," and she was determined to advocate those rights. At a Labor Day celebration that year she urged labor groups to unite in their support of a constitution that would foster humane legislation for "children, the aged, and the infirm."

As a national observer later noted, ". . . here was a woman who had the wit, which others had not, to grasp the opportunity offered by the constitution of a new and promising commonwealth. . . ." Barnard was determined that, unlike so many other states, Oklahoma would not later see her newly drafted reform legislation declared unconstitutional. Instead, the new constitution would be based on a philosophy of reform.

As a delegate from the Woman's Union Label League, she went to Shawnee that fall to help draft Labor's 24 Demands, a platform that the territorial Federation of Labor, the railroad brotherhoods, and the Farmers' Union hoped to make a part of the new constitution. The 24 Demands included provisions for child labor laws, compulsory education, inspections of mines, an 8-hour day on all public work, and a corporate commission to regulate business and adjudicate disputes in industrial regulatory matters. The union leaders also wanted a suffrage plank, though the Democrats of the state did not support such a plank. Barnard herself was neutral on the issue in the beginning, probably because of her father's great opposition to the vote for women.

The group sent its 24 Demands to candidates of both parties, asking for a pledge of support. Kate Barnard then stumped the territory, making 44 speeches in the weeks before the November 6 election. Describing the poverty and injustice that she had observed in other states, she urged the people of the Twin Territories to elect men who would draft a constitution based on the 24 Demands, so that the very foundations of state government would recognize the rights of working men and women. For "until Society is just to its working men, it cannot expect its workers to be just and honorable in their individual lives," she said. She argued that the only way "to stamp out poverty, with its resultant degradation and crime, is to begin with the children," and she explained that she wanted a child labor plank in the constitution because, without such a plank, proving the constitutionality of a child labor act would take years, and "we can't waste children for years."

The people listened to her arguments, and when the votes were counted, it was evident that the labor-farmer coalition that she had helped to unify had held firm. A Democratic landslide ensued, and the constitutional convention that convened at Guthrie on November 20, 1906, was controlled by those who had endorsed the 24 Demands.

Though Barnard had no possibility of becoming an official delegate to that all-male convention, her influence was strongly evident there. She had researched laws from other states and used her research to draft the constitutional planks she advocated. Then, on December 5, 1906, she did what she did best—she gave a rousing speech against long hours, unsanitary workshops, and child labor, a speech that was later described as "one of the notable events of that historic body." There is no mistaking the power of her appeal:

> If you farmers vote for child labor in this state, I hope that in the fall of the year when the sap goes out of your cornstalks and leaves the stalks dry and dead and rasping and bare, that God will turn your cornstalks into the skeletons of little children and shake their dry bones at you.

In the face of such oratory, the delegates made Oklahoma's the first constitution to be drafted with a plank regulating child labor.

By mid-March, 1907, 10 of the original 24 articles had been adopted, and one of those articles created the office of commissioner of Charities and Corrections, an office that could be held by man or woman and was clearly designed with Kate Barnard in mind. In an eloquent speech to the assembled delegates, Barnard congratulated them for drafting a constitution that laid the basis for laws that would protect working-class citizens and urged them to fight for its ratification and for the adoption of laws that would convert its ideals into realities.

It was the longest constitution ever drafted by a modern democracy. More important, imperfect as it was, it presented a very real threat to conservative Republicans, and they sought to have Congress declare the newly drafted document invalid. Barnard went to the National Conference of Charities in Minneapolis that summer to alert her reformer friends that "all the powers of darkness" were set upon destroying "this document, which contains more of human liberty than anything written since the Declaration of Independence." She urged them to write, telegram, or speak directly to the president on behalf of the Oklahoma constitution. Barnard's speech was a masterpiece, and one delegate declared he hadn't seen such emotion worked in 15 years of conferences. When later asked to comment upon accusations that she worked on the emotions of her hearers, Barnard replied that that was exactly what she always intended to do.

While Barnard was in Minneapolis, the Democratic state convention met and nominated her for the office of commissioner of Charities and Corrections. Though her father, feeling a woman's place was in the home, disapproved of her increasing involvement in politics, she accepted the nomination and began her campaign for the election in which the people of Twin Territories would accept or reject the constitution and elect their first slate of state officials.

The campaigning was colorful and intense, and Barnard was a clear platform favorite. When the votes were in she had defeated her Republican opponent by over 35,000 votes; she had drawn more votes than any other candidate for state office. Her victory made her the first woman in the United States to be elected to a statewide office by an all-male electorate.

At this point in her career, Barnard was not yet a supporter of woman's suffrage, for, as she said, "the boys have always done what [I] asked them to do without [my] needing any vote for [myself]." She was later to regret such flippancy, and to the end of her career she was haunted by the warning of a suffragist, ". . . those for whom you have toiled and with whom you have worked will prove ungrateful, and you will more fully understand the necessity of women of Oklahoma having the direct power of the ballot."

But in 1907 Barnard had not yet tasted betrayal, and her plea was for united effort in the work of building a new state, asserting that "Men have reason and aggression; women, intuition, sentiment, ideas, and tact. Together they succeed." True to this belief, she chose a male, Hobart Huson, as assistant director of her department and named a female, Estella Blair, as departmental secretary. She described Huson, the journalist who had shared her experiences in St. Louis, as an "intellectual nomad" ready to give all to "a Work of Love for Humanity in the State House of Oklahoma." The alliance was to prove a favorable one for the department, for Huson was as dedicated to the work as she was.

Having chosen her staff, Barnard set out with enthusiasm to fulfill the rather staggering duties of her new office:

> to investigate the entire system of public charities and corrections, to examine into the condition and management of all prisons, jails, almshouses, reformatories, reform and industrial schools, hospitals, infirmatories, dispensaries, orphanages, and all public and private retreats and asylums. . . .

Although she had learned much about such work from her experiences in St. Louis and Chicago, she realized that with only her own limited knowledge and experience to guide her, she would be performing her varied and complex duties largely on a trial-and-error basis and that such an approach was wasteful and likely to lead to failure. She therefore launched an innovative program in which she invited the nation's leading experts on social welfare issues—juvenile delinquency, prison reform, child labor, mental health—to come to Oklahoma to speak to the public and to the legislature. She even called upon some of these experts to give direct help in the drafting of reform legislation. This was a logical administrative procedure, and one practiced in business ventures, yet it had no precedent in government councils. Barnard herself gave her innovative method a name. She called it "Scientific Statecraft" and defined it as simply the use of "the experts of the nation to draft . . . laws for the helpless; to avoid the mistakes of older states and include the most advanced and humane thought. . . ."

Through this "Scientific Statecraft" she roused public and legislative sympathy for the reforms she supported. But her own accounts of her investigations were as effective in her cause as the speeches and articles of the experts. She described for Oklahomans the life led by children in the cotton mills:

> silenced by the deafening roar of the machinery, and stifled by the hot steam and lint-laden air—long rows of little, old, thin-chested, stoop-shouldered, sallow-cheeked, leaden-eyed, pipe-stem figures hurrying back and forth before the flying shuttle. . . . [The] vitality of these children should not be expended in the morning of their lives, leaving them physical degenerates . . . listless and helpless to wander on over the desert of their wrecked and ruined careers.

Barnard campaigned tirelessly, but the battle for legislation proved to be much harder than the battle for constitutional planks, and it was not until 1909 that a bill giving Oklahoma one of the toughest child labor provisions in the nation was signed into law. Later Barnard declared that on the day the governor signed the child labor bill into law, "eight hundred children came out of the black pits of Oklahoma, five hundred more were released from the laundries of the state, and thousands more were liberated in miscellaneous industries."

Thanks largely to Barnard's efforts, the constitution held a compulsory education plank, and she set out to pass legislation ensuring at least a rudimentary education so that ". . . the Bible and the best literature shall not be to them forever a sealed book." Her campaigning helped pass a compulsory education bill stating that Oklahoma's children, ages 8 to 16, were to be in school 3 to 6 months of each year.

With characteristic understanding of the plight of the poor, she helped add a radical clause to that 1908 law, a clause providing a "scholarship fund" that paid to widowed mothers the wages that their dependent children would have earned had they been working, rather than in school. Though this was a relatively costly provision, she managed to convince the legislators that it was a highly economical one, since the "true wealth of the nation must be figured in terms of child-life" and "a dollar spent in the morning of their lives is better than a thousand spent in the evening—in shelters called poorhouses."

She continued her fight for children's rights, speaking around the country on behalf of child labor laws, helping to found the Southern Conference on Woman and Child Labor, and pushing for the creation of the National Children's Bureau.*

Her concern for the welfare of children was evident in her work for an Oklahoma juvenile justice system that would separate youthful offenders from hardened criminals and provide for them a greater chance for reform. Horrified to find that more than 800 children under age 16 were in jail, while 60 more were in the penitentiary, most for trivial offenses, she drafted a bill that made a firm distinction between deliquent children and adult criminals and made provisions for separation of the 2 classes of offenders.

Ideally, Barnard wanted a system of reformatories designed to hold young offenders until they had completed a vocational rehabilitation program that would provide them with a trade through which they could obtain gainful employment. And she wanted to establish well-staffed orphans' homes for dependent and neglected children who might otherwise soon fall into a life of petty crime, for she knew that many workers in existing institutions found it "much easier to beat a child than to mold a life through kindness and fair treatment." Inspired by her meetings with other reformers, her vision of these institutions anticipated the most modern theories of juvenile correction.

She felt an equal concern for adult prisoners, a concern greatly heightened by her direct observation of the inhumane conditions under which they were confined. Within 6 months of taking office, she and Huson had inspected 61 county jails, condemning two-thirds of them for unsanitary and overcrowded conditions and/or for the immoral, inhumane behavior of the sheriffs.

---

* That bureau, established in 1912 and dedicated to the investigation of "all matters pertaining to the welfare of children," became, in 1953, the Department of Health, Education, and Welfare (HEW).

Barnard described model centers—clean, sanitary cells, well-lighted, well-ventilated, and provided with proper bathing and toilet facilities. Further, she maintained that no prisoner should be long detained even in such a model jail, urging speedy trials that would free the innocent and sentence the guilty to terms in the penitentiary or other appropriate corrections facilities.

Unfortunately, the fledgling state had no penitentiary of its own and, under a contractual agreement, sent its prisoners to the Kansas State Penitentiary at Lansing, or, in the case of Indians, to the federal penitentiary at Leavenworth. After hearing countless complaints about the Lansing facility, Barnard and her assistant made an unannounced visit there in August of 1908. Paying the 10-cent admission fee, they made the standard public tour of the facility without revealing their identity; then, armed with their findings from this cursory inspection, they went to the warden to demand an official inspection.

After making her rounds through cells, hospital, and kitchen, through the mines, the brick works, and the contract-labor furniture factory, Barnard concluded that "the state of Kansas was spending something like a half million dollars a year in the manufacture of monsters." In the "hole," or dungeon, she found a 17-year-old Oklahoma boy strung up in irons for failure to meet his 3-car-per-day quota of coal. As she later recalled, "He told me with tears in his eyes, that he had gotten out a little over two cars but that he just could not get anymore." Though the boy had never dug coal before his prison term, his quota was equal to that of experienced miners.

Arguing that a weaker man was more likely than not to become "slave of a slave in a dark hole in a mine," and that men had been known to kill each other over a carload of coal, she urged that the quota system be altered to suit the skills of the workers and insisted that young boys should never be sent into the mines at all. Convinced that contract-labor systems, whether with state-owned or privately owned industries, encouraged abuse of prisoners, she and Huson took careful note of the quotas demanded of all the men in the mines and of the unsafe conditions under which they toiled.

Calling upon her own governor and the governor of Kansas to

launch a full-scale investigation, she returned home to prepare her own notes on the state penitentiary at Lansing. She brought a group of 5 former Oklahoma inmates to testify at the hearing, and though newspapers called the men "Kate's band of murderers," their testimony was allowed to stand.

The investigation at Lansing sent shock waves far beyond the 2 states directly involved in the scandal. Great concern for prison reform was generated across the country, and Barnard was called upon to address state and national meetings over the next few years. Her speeches were convincing, and reforms in several other states, notably Arizona and Arkansas, can be traced directly to her influence.

In an article printed in the *New York Times* in 1912, Barnard maintained that "high and strong as their walls might be, prisons which failed to reform failed to protect society against crime." She argued that there was "too much 'charity' in our present system . . . [and] too little economic justice," so that the course the prisoners took when released "is, more likely than not, as bad as, or worse than, the way they followed before they got in."

Her hope was to develop a system in which prisoners would be trained to follow a pattern very similar to that which they would be expected to follow in the outside world. For his work, each prisoner would be paid wages commensurate with those of the outside world, and those wages would be used in the support of his family. Further, every prisoner would receive some form of education—in a trade or in basic skills—and the honor system, enforced by much encouragement for achievement, would prevail.

These were ideas far ahead of her time. But most of Barnard's program of reform was based on concepts that would not be accepted for years to come. As early as 1913 she was citing poverty as a major cause of crime. While acknowledging that the poverty that made humans desperate enough to steal could be rooted in a personal fault such as laziness or drunkenness, she avowed that crime was more often caused by social ills such as unemployment and long hours and low wages.

In an attempt to cure the ill of unemployment, she organized state-operated employment agencies, which, at no charge, tried to fit the employee to the job. To cure the ill of long hours and low wages she helped pass laws preventing discrimination against union workers.

In addition, Barnard fought for the physical and mental health of Oklahoma's citizens. She appointed a state factory inspector and fought for laws guaranteeing safe working conditions in the mines. She defeated a bond issue that would have created a water supply dam fed by a river dangerously polluted by Oklahoma City's untreated sewage. After visiting model mental institutions in other states, she fought for laws that would prevent the mentally ill from being treated as criminals and would guarantee them modern, efficient treatment facilities. She worked to provide schools and homes for the blind, the deaf, and the mentally retarded, as well as for orphans.

Of particular concern to her was the problem of orphaned Indian minors. In fall of 1909, after she and her assistant Huson had managed to track down the three "elf children" rumored to be living in a hollow tree, they spent nearly 6 weeks tracking down the court-appointed guardian who was legally responsible for the welfare of these Indian orphans. To their astonishment, they found this man had 51 other Indian children under his care, yet he had lost track of them all.

Unfortunately, this situation was all too common. In Oklahoma, county judges were empowered to appoint guardians for orphaned Indian minors. Many of the orphans had inherited oil-rich lands, and these holdings made the children attractive prey for those who coveted their oil and coal rights. Court-appointed guardians were authorized to sell the land "for benefit of the minor," but the minor rarely benefited from such sales. Guardians regularly pocketed profits, claiming that most of the money they gained from the sale of land and mineral rights had gone into court costs and attorneys' fees, while the balance was "safely invested."

Horrified by their discovery of such injustice, Barnard and Huson asked the state to name their department "next friend" of Indian minors, a designation that gave them a legal mandate to intervene in any transactions affecting the rights of these children. A bill was passed giving Barnard's department the right to interfere on behalf of orphaned minors in state homes. When an emergency bill granted her an additional staff member, an inspector, she gave the job to a lawyer, J. H. Stolper, and put him in charge of investigations on behalf of defrauded Indian children. One after another, Stolper brought the guardians to trial; by 1912 he had helped over 1,350 orphans to recover nearly one million dollars—at a total cost to the state of less than $6,000.

But Stolper's convictions crossed party lines. They involved Democrats as often as Republicans and implicated prominent judges who had awarded promising guardianships to their political supporters. Stolper, Barnard, and Huson were making political enemies in the guardianship cases. When the plight of children, of laborers, even of prisoners had been her concern, Barnard had enjoyed public support, for thousands of voters cared deeply about children, laborers, and prisoners. But who cared for the rights of orphaned Indians? Even Oklahoma's poor were, at best, indifferent, and, at worst, openly hostile to Indian issues. In the opinion of one newspaper editor:

> Sympathy and sentiment never stand in the way of the onward march of empire. If the Indians don't learn the value of property and how to adjust themselves to surroundings, they will be "grafted" out of it—that is one of the unchangeable laws of God and the constitution of man.

That editorial likely mirrored public sentiment, and Barnard could find no statewide base of support for her crusade, nothing save her own firm conviction of the immorality of seizing lands from the children she called "a weak and helpless remnant of a race which once possessed the American continent."

Despite this lack of sympathy and support, she managed to continue prosecution of dishonest guardians. When funding became a problem, she diverted most of her general operating funds into this work. Unable to stop Stolper in any other way, enemies accused him of accepting money in return for using his influence to protect bootleggers. There was apparently enough truth in those charges to force Stolper to resign from office in early 1913.

That November, devastated by the loss of her legal adviser and disillusioned by what she saw as man's inhumanity to man, Barnard appealed to the women of the state, telling a group of Muskogee suffragists that "Men do not know how to safeguard the human race, they have had the opportunity for two thousand years and have failed. . . . Women seek the ballot only that the race may develop and go forward. . . . drop this cry of woman's rights, ours is a struggle for human rights."

That struggle had taken its toll on Kate Barnard. Although she continued her investigations into Indian minor frauds, she was not able to work at full efficiency. Her mental and physical health had steadily deteriorated; she was no longer the powerful little woman whose strength of will had swayed thousands.

From the earliest days of her public life Barnard had tended to take no thought for her own need to rest, working until she collapsed, then attributing her collapse to flu, pneumonia, or exhaustion. The death of her father in May of 1909 was a heavy blow. "I am broken in health and my heart is consumed with grief," she wrote a friend. "I do not know whether I will ever be able to continue the good work I have begun." Later that same year she expressed to the governor her frustration at "wear[ing] . . . [her] nervous system out securing laws and appropriations," only to see the work thwarted by petty political bickering.

From that date her frustrations seemed to mount. She was a dream weaver who believed in her own dreams and made others believe in them, too. But when the dreams took longer to realize than she had anticipated, disillusionment set in. Despite all her efforts, children were still hungry, prisoners were still being abused, the mentally ill were still being treated as criminals.

A year after John Barnard's death, his daughter, wearied by a strenuous political campaign in support of fellow Democrats while maintaining her already difficult schedule, was ordered to take a rest. She spent some time in a sanitarium in the Colorado Rockies, returning to wage a successful fight for her own reelection and to give renewed energy to the Indian minors issue. But her stamina and her recuperative abilities grew weaker with each successive period of collapse, and her chance for permanent recovery was lessened by her inability to withdraw completely and recover fully before reentering the fray.

She was out of her office for nearly 6 months in 1911 and again for a considerable portion of 1912. At this point, the true nature of her illness could no longer be hidden from the public, and a *New York Herald Tribune* article of August 1913 declared that she had suffered a complete nervous breakdown.

The breakdown, first evidenced in April, was likely triggered by the vote of censure of Barnard, Huson, and Stolper passed by the House Committee on Efficiency. Officially, that censure came because of their repeated and extended absences from the department offices, though the real reason for the censure was their refusal to drop their work on behalf of the Indian minors.

The committee had actually recommended that the Department of Charities and Corrections be abolished and its duties subsumed under other branches of government, but the legislature could not legally abolish an office created by the constitution. Thwarted, the lawmakers decided to destroy Barnard's effectiveness by underfunding her work. The House slashed her operating funds and eliminated two staff positions, leaving her with only a secretary.

By early 1914, she realized her power in the Oklahoma statehouse was spent, and she decided against running for a third term of office. Instead, she gave her energy to organizing a People's Lobby to influence government policy. Barnard's old charisma was still evident, and the People's Lobby campaigned successfully against many candidates hostile to her reform measures.

Meantime, Barnard continued her battle against the Indian guardianship fraud. From a group of reformers outside the state she received $10,000 to publicize the plight of Indians in Oklahoma. She made Hobart Huson, her long-time friend, head of the campaign, and headquarters opened in late June of 1914. The $10,000 was used up within six months, but Barnard fought on, her efforts drawing national attention through articles in the *New York Times* and other major newspapers. In March of 1915, in an unprecedented move, she spoke on the floor of the Oklahoma Senate, a place where no woman had stood before, pleading the cause of Indian minors. But the Oklahoma legislators were deaf to her eloquence. In April of 1916 she made her last attempt to end the evil. She wrote to President Wilson, describing her largely futile battle to aid the Indians and asking him to consider resumption of federal jurisdiction over them. Kate Barnard then sank out of sight, her spirit and her health broken at last.

Having given her last bit of energy to an unpopular cause, Barnard succumbed to the mental and physical ills that had plagued her for years. Her collapse may have been influenced by her discovery that Hobart Huson, her untiring assistant and a man she once said must be named "among the human lives most close to mine," had early on deserted a wife and 2 sons. Entirely disillusioned, Barnard now withdrew from public life, and the boundless energy and ceaseless attention to detail that had made her work for others so effective was given over to an endless contemplation of her own condition. She saw herself as a victim of "the hypocrisy, deceit, selfishness, and intrigue of modern politics." In an unpublished autobiographical fragment written during these years, she lamented, "the best years of my life and the best Service of my life [are] lost to the World."

Her morbid preoccupation with her physical ills and her endless concentration upon the wrongs that had been dealt her made her bitter and unstable. Three months before her fifty-fifth birthday, on February 23, 1930, death ended the pain of the helplessness. A maid found her body in the Oklahoma City hotel suite that had been her home for several years. The end had come peacefully through heart failure.

The estrangement of the intervening years was momentarily forgotten, and the "Good Angel of Oklahoma" was given fitting honors. On the day of her funeral, the state flag was lowered to half-mast and all 7 of the men who had served Oklahoma as governor were honorary pallbearers. Fourteen hundred people gathered at St. Joseph's Cathedral to hear her eulogy, and many of them were present to see her casket lowered into the grave beside her father's tomb, the tomb on which she had had engraved "Every good deed of my life I dedicate to him, and my one ambition is to live a life worthy of his name." Her own grave remained unmarked until 1982, when a small stone bearing the inscription "Intrepid pioneer leader for social ethics in Oklahoma" was placed there by a group determined to give Kate Barnard the honor she had earned through her service to her state.

Though her name was all but forgotten for over 50 years, the influence of Kate Barnard's work far outlived her. She had once described that work as being "a prayerful attempt to reach and remedy . . . wrongs, to bring comfort and security where I had found mortgages, rags, hunger, and despair. . . ." With unbelievable skill she had helped to mold a constitution that set the stage for innovative, effective social legislation. She brought to the attention of an entire nation the plight of laborers, prisoners, and the children of the poor. Through the practice of "Scientific Statecraft," she used the experiences of others to avoid inefficient trial-and-error bureaucracy. With a minuscule staff and limited funds, she achieved more in her first 6 months of elected office than most well-staffed, well-funded agencies accomplish in 6 years of effort.

In 1907 she had told a reporter, "I hope by my example to show what any girl from the commonest walks of life can do for suffering humanity if she will really, earnestly try." All of her early achievements seemed to show how worthy an example she was, and these early successes seemed to point toward even greater accomplishments. But such was not to be the case. When progress slowed to a normal pace, when the overnight changes ceased and her work began to plod rather than to leap forward, when the praise and support grew weak and the opposition and criticism grew strong, she was too impatient, too idealistic, too sensitive to adjust. At one time she had been philosophical about such frustrations, saying that what counted was "throwing little pebbles in the great ocean of human events—making ripples." Kate Barnard had thrown those pebbles and made those ripples.

·~· *Williamina Fleming* ·~·
A Field for Woman's Work

*T*he large, sturdily built man of handsome patrician aspect leaned forward and gently replaced the phone on its hook. "It's likely to take her a little while now," he said to the younger man sitting across the desk from him. "You know, this has really caught her interest."

"But, Doctor, if it's as she says it is, I can't account for it . . . it doesn't fit." Henry Russell was stunned, impatient, yet unwilling to betray his impatience to the kindly scholar who was offering him all the resources of the observatory to identify his surprising find.

"Well, it is as she says it is, Doctor, I'll stake my reputation on that. In fact," he added with a bemused smile, "I've staked my reputation on her for a quarter of a century now." Edward Charles Pickering leaned back in his chair and glanced at his visitor, a man

*who, in his early thirties, was already an astronomer of some re-
nown.*

*"I know, sir, I've heard," Russell answered, his tone betraying the
respect he held for both the director of the Harvard College Observatory and the woman who had worked so zealously with him in
establishing its preeminent position. "A quarter of a century?"*

*"Well, even longer, I suppose. She came in '79. But she didn't take
over right away, you know. . . . I had to teach her a few things
first."*

*Pickering was obviously enjoying himself now. He settled in the
chair and let the memories sweep over him. He felt better talking
of his assistant. His assistant? His colleague! Talking somehow
vented the frustration he'd felt as he'd watched her strength wane
over the last few months. Heaven knew he couldn't talk of it much
with her. All his attempts to convince her to shorten her hours, cut
back her schedule were rebuffed by the redoubtable lady who
pushed on with the monumental work at hand.*

*Catching Pickering's mood, Russell gave his senior the lead.
"Well, you taught her well, Doctor, there's no one going to deny
that."*

*"Yes, I taught her. Brought her in here one day because I knew
she was what the place needed. I'm embarrassed to tell you this"—
Pickering glanced quickly at Russell—"she was my housemaid, you
know."*

"I know, Doctor."

*"She was doing domestic work—with her mind and her spirit,
doing domestic work for the Pickerings." He was almost ignoring his
visitor now, speaking more to himself than to another presence. "She
was just over here, new to the country, a young thing, 21 maybe;
she'd just left her husband and she needed the money. She was
supporting herself and expecting at the time. Anyway, we'd just
begun the program and we got behind down here—just a staff of
4 and they couldn't handle all we were giving them. I knew we
could use her, thought she'd be perfect—little did I know how perfect. That was '79. Two years later she was full-time permanent
staff, and 4 years later, when we were setting up the Draper*

Memorial, she took charge. That's been hers almost from the start . . . I mean, sometimes I think I get in her way."

Pickering smiled to himself and fell silent. His whiskered chin rested now on hands templed under it. Russell let the silence stand. He already knew Mina Fleming's background and, besides, he was too concerned about her present activity to be diverted to a history of her past.

Silence sat between them, the older man caught in his reverie and the younger man sorting through the implications of Fleming's search. The harsh jab of the phone brought both men back to the moment.

Pickering made no move toward the instrument, motioning instead for his visitor to lift the receiver. "Dr. Pickering's office," Russell said, then silence. "A? You're sure, Mrs. Fleming? And the others are all G?"

His mood broken by the obvious excitement shared by Henry Russell and Mina Fleming, Dr. Pickering sat forward again.

"That's something new then. . . . What do you think?" Russell's face was alive with the news. "Fine, fine. . . . well, thank you."

Second-guessing Mina Fleming's answers, Edward Pickering rose to offer his hand to the young astronomer. "Well, now your real work begins," he said with a chuckle. "Now, how will you make your theory conform to our reality?"

The year was 1910, and Russell later wrote of this moment, "The first person who knew of the existence of white dwarfs was Mrs. Fleming, the next two . . . Professor E. C. Pickering and I."

Mrs. Fleming, the object of Professor Pickering's reverie and Dr. Russell's admiration, was in fact the first person to know not only of white dwarfs, stars of incredible density, but of many other celestial wonders. At her death she had the rare distinction of having discovered more stars than any other person in the history of the world. And she had the equally rare distinction of being the first woman ever to hold an official position at Harvard University.

Williamina Paton Stevens was born in Dundee, Scotland, on May 15, 1857. Though few details of her early life survive, it is known that she came from the sturdiest stock of the nation. Her mother was a Graham, a name that rings in Scottish history. Her father, a skilled craftsman, had settled with his young wife in the port city of Dundee, where he established a carving and a gilding business. He was greatly interested in a new invention being talked of on the continent, a process called "photography." It is said that Robert Stevens experimented with photography and was the first to introduce the daguerrotype process to Dundee.

Though Mina Fleming may have received her enthusiasm for scientific investigation from her father, her memories of him were necessarily vague, for he died when she was 7 years old. Left with several young children in her care, Mina's mother attempted to keep the framing shop open, but eventually closed its doors. How she provided thereafter is not known, but Mina assumed her share of responsibility early in life. She attended the local public school and at 14 became a pupil-teacher at Broughton-Ferry, a village on the outskirts of Dundee. She continued her own education in this manner for the next 5 years.

In 1877 at age 20 she married James Fleming. The promise of America lured the young couple, and they sailed from Dundee, arriving in Boston late in 1878. For reasons unknown, Mina Fleming's marriage ended shortly after her arrival here. Thrown on her own resources and aware that she was expecting a child, she found employment as the second maid in the household of Edward Pickering.

An industrious young woman, ambitious and inordinately bright, she quickly caught the fancy of the professor and his wife, a childless couple. It was a particularly auspicious time in the lives of the Pickerings. Just 2 years prior, at the age of 31 and over some rather strong objections, Dr. Pickering had been appointed to the directorship of the observatory. With a doctorate in physics and a reputation as an outstanding instructor at Massachusetts Institute of Technology, Pickering found his appointment opposed by those who thought the position of director of a major observatory should be reserved for an "observational astronomer."

But Edward C. Pickering was a young man with ideas, and his

acceptance of the position was to prove fortuitous, not only for the Harvard College Observatory, but for the development of astronomy itself. From the first, he determined a new course for the observatory, one that would lead it into the new age of astrophysical investigation.

In the last half of the nineteenth century, astronomy, although one of the oldest fields of human investigation, was still not considered a pure science. Rather it was looked upon as a practical arm of the physical sciences. It was used to provide such necessary services as determining accurate time, establishing latitude and longitude, and setting geographical boundaries. But there were stirrings, developments in peripheral fields that foreshadowed major advances in astronomy.

Astronomy was not yet a pure science because it was necessarily such a subjective science. Its pursuit had been limited by the disproportionate relationship between the scope of the heavens and the power of man's meager tools of exploration. From the days of antiquity humans had sought to measure the sky. The first known list of the stars was made about 150 B.C. by Hipparchus, an illustrious Greek astronomer. That list gave the position and comparative brightness—as estimated by Hipparchus—of several hundred stars. Some 3 centuries later, Ptolemy of Alexandria gave the world the concept of a sun-centered universe and advanced the catalog of stars to more than 1,000. The stars were listed by name and position and were divided into 6 groups according to their relative brilliance. The brightest stars were said to be of the first magnitude, the faintest were assigned to the sixth magnitude.

The Ptolemaic list sufficed for the centuries that intervened before the invention of the telescope introduced new horizons. Now 100,000 stars could be seen and identified. In 1863 the monumental *Bonner Durchmusterung* (*The Bonn Catalogue*) was issued and quickly became the standard work in its field; it listed the position and magnitude of 300,000 stars. But the structure of the stars was still only a matter of conjecture, and their classification by brilliance was still dependent upon the sight, judgment, and experience of the individual observer. As might be imagined, the collection of celestial facts by visual observation was slow and inaccurate. Then in the nineteenth century the science of astronomy was stirred by significant developments in two other fields. The first occurred with the invention and the refinement of photographic techniques that, when applied to astronomy, meant that celestial observation no longer depended upon one isolated individual's fleeting glimpse of a star. Now celestial phenomena could be recorded for study and comparison.

In 1850 a photograph of the moon taken and developed on a daguerrotype plate at the Harvard College Observatory was considered so spectacular that it was placed on display at the International Exhibition being held in London that year. The use of photography boded a new future in systematic astronomical research. For the next decade, the Harvard observatory was the center of experimentation in celestial photography. But because of inherent difficulties in the process and lack of dedication and funds, further work was eventually suspended.

In the meantime, advances were being made in a related field. A great deal of information about the brightness, position, and distance of the stars could be obtained with the aid of the telescope and the telescopic camera. But the composition of the star, its temperature, and its speed and direction of movement remained major, disturbing mysteries. Then, almost concurrently with the development of photography, a new science evolved, the science of spectroscopy.

Here, a prism placed before the lens of the telescope caught not a point of light, but the spectrum emitted by the light. Now stars could be seen as tiny strips of a rainbow, a colorful image that, once decoded, could tell a full and fascinating story. If its spectrum could be known, then so too could a star's chemistry, its temperature, and its direction and speed of movement. The time was ripe for new and remarkable advances in stellar investigation.

It was at this time that the work of the Harvard College Observatory was placed in the hands of a man who could appreciate the promise held by application of these new tools and new methods to astronomy.

The directorship of the observatory had been turned down by several men before it was offered to Pickering—men who saw that the observatory was "poor in means, meager in instruments, wanting in assistants" and concluded that there seemed "little prospect of doing much." Pickering, on the other hand, saw vast prospects. Harvard Observatory had an established reputation; given new energy and direction, it could become a leader in the astrophysical movement.

Pickering began with a 3-year program that devoted his energies and those of his staff to the new field of photometry, or the measurement of the brilliance of the stars. The project entailed prolonged observation and classification of relative brilliance as determined by an exact standard. To do this, Pickering devised revolutionary new equipment, and he adopted as the base of comparison of stellar brilliance a magnitude scale first proposed at Oxford a quarter of a century earlier.

This ambitious program soon generated volumes of data, all of which had to be copied and computed. Copying and computing was painstaking work. The staff of the computer room made note of each star, then identified and calculated its celestial position. There were no calculating machines available, and all computations were carried out with paper and pencil, the chief aid being a table of logarithms. The work was slow and tedious, and the staff fell farther and farther behind.

Having noted the efficiency and intelligence shown by his helper at home, Dr. Pickering soon pressed Mrs. Fleming into service at the observatory. That simple, momentary necessity was the inauspicious beginning of a brilliant career in science.

In the early days, Fleming worked only in the observatory as needed, and she was assigned only the simplest computing and recording chores. But she lent even to these tasks the attention to detail that was to mark all her work.

Early in the fall of 1879 Mina Fleming returned to Dundee to give birth to her child, a son whom she named Edward Pickering Fleming. But her loyalty to Pickering and her vision of a fulfilling life in America soon brought her and her infant back to Boston.

There she returned to work for the Pickerings, alternately at home and at the observatory. However, the professor's need for her in the computing room soon began to consume more and more of her time, and by 1881 she was made a full-time member of the permanent staff at the observatory.

In the dispatch of her routine computations, Mina Fleming showed such a capacity for original observation that she was gradually assigned more difficult and more responsible tasks. Impressed by her work, Pickering began to give her instruction, extending her knowledge in the concepts of mathematics and physics that lay behind stellar investigation. By the time Pickering issued his first report of the photometric project, Fleming was in charge of the observatory's computing staff.

"It was only necessary to tell her exactly what was needed, and she saw that it was carried through successfully in every detail," Pickering later wrote of Fleming's administrative ability. Mina Fleming was a no-nonsense administrator. She set high standards for those who worked for her, and she expected compliance. She imposed efficient methods and she expected trustworthy results. She was an administrator who evoked awe and respect from those who worked with her or under her.

By 1883, Pickering was beginning to give voice to a new ambition— one that was to lead to one of the most fruitful scientific projects of the time. He wished to produce a photographic map of the sky, and toward this end he planned an elaborate program of celestial photography. It was an expensive undertaking, and an 1886 windfall greatly enhanced the work. The widow of Henry Draper, the man who had pioneered in stellar spectral photography, decided to donate his equpiment, his accumulated records, and a monthly stipend to Harvard College Observatory in order that her husband's work might be carried on. Systematic astronomic research now began in earnest under the auspices of the Henry Draper Memorial. A permanent record of celestial phenomena was assured, and spectral photography, through which the makeup of the heavens could be made known, was brought into the sphere of academic investigation.

Pickering, in effect, now instituted a systematic patrol of the skies.

He began by adapting the physical arrangement of the observatory to a photographic operation. Every clear night a telescopic camera recorded conditions in a portion of the sky 10 degrees square. The brightness of a star was photographed as a point (with a telescope moved by clockwork), as a line (with a telescope held stationary for the length of the camera's exposure), or as a spectrum (with a prism placed before the telescopic camera lens). All the stars visible in the field impressed themselves as points, lines, or spectra simultaneously on the plate. Each plate was given two exposures, one early in the evening and one in the late night sky.

Every morning the plates were carried in light-proof boxes to the developing cottage. There each photograph was etched on a glass plate 8 × 10 inches in size. These brittle, fragile records, each containing the spectra of a large number of stars, were then placed in the hands of copyists and computers. From the plates, mounted for examination under bright daylight, the position, brightness, variability, and color of each star could be determined. The examination of the plates, the measurement of the position and brightness of the stars shown thereon, and the cataloging of the results obtained from those plates fell upon Mina Fleming and the trained staff of assistants.

It was a period of rapid development at the observatory. In early 1887, Pickering, more and more engrossed in administration and fund-raising, assigned the management of the Henry Draper Memorial to Mina Fleming. It was a formidable responsibility. The average number of photographs taken annually reached 2,000, and each photograph had to be examined, analyzed, indexed, and stored so as to be instantly available for later reference.

As the volume and significance of the work grew more immense, Fleming's position and talents grew more indispensable to the task. Her keen skills in observation, her ability to think quickly and logically proved invaluable in the organization of the material that began to accumulate. "She possessed a remarkable memory and a gift for order and system," Pickering later recalled in attempting to explain her accomplishments.

The detailed survey of the celestial regions made accessible by telescopic photography soon yielded an amount of data that defied any extant system of stellar classification. Hitherto, astronomers around the world had accepted a system of classification that assigned each star observed to one of four spectral groups, using the sun's spectrum as the standard. But now Pickering and Fleming could enlarge by 5 times a spectral image less than ½″ long, and such highly defined spectra demanded a more sophisticated system of classification.

Pickering devised a new system; Fleming modified and expanded it. The Pickering-Fleming system allowed for 17 different categories of spectral classification; the categories were named by letters of the alphabet from A to Q. Over 99 percent of the stars observed fell into 6 classes—A, B, F, G, K, and M. Q was reserved for those stars showing a peculiar spectrum that defied any other classifications, and those that fell under Q were noted as objects of special interest for further study.*

At the beginning of the last decade of the nineteenth century, with classification of the stars in the northern hemisphere well underway, Pickering established an observatory near Arequipa in Peru for the purpose of surveying the dome of the southern hemisphere. The photographic plates taken at that station were routinely shipped to the Harvard observatory, there to be examined and added to the growing library.

Mina Fleming found herself in a unique position. She was involved in work for which there was no precedent. And she evinced a special talent for that work. The minute inspection of this wonderful collection of photographs, "charts covering an entire sky from the north to the south pole," afforded a great opportunity for original investigation and consequent discovery of new celestial bodies. The secrets that those plates yielded to the patient scrutiny of Mina Fleming and to her finely developed instinct for interpreting data came to constitute an unparalleled record of discovery. If there was a spectrum among the hundreds of lines on a plate that hadn't ap-

---

* The Pickering-Fleming system was later refined by Annie Jump Cannon of Harvard. Cannon's rearrangement became the definitive system of spectral classification.

peared before, she detected it. Among changing stars she caught hundreds in the act of changing. Should a bright star suddenly appear in the sky, she documented its previous condition from the growing library of photographic plates.

The work of the Draper Memorial began in 1886, and by 1890 an immense collection of photographs of stellar spectra had been gathered. The data revealed by the study of those plates was published in 1890 as the *Draper Catalog of Stellar Spectra.* It was, for its time, the definitive catalog of the stars, a comprehensive, comparative study of 10,351 stars down to the eighth magnitude, and the first published attempt to establish the structure of celestial bodies. "A general index to the physical nature of 10,000 objects is a novelty of first importance," one colleague noted. The publication of the *Draper Catalogue,* for which Professor Pickering gave Mina Fleming full credit, was a signal event in the history of astronomy.

Mina Fleming was now directing an all-woman team of 18 computers, she was making daily decisions in the indexing and cataloging of photographic plates, and she was deducing facts of wonderful accuracy and interest. According to the official history of the Harvard College Observatory,

> Among the many thousands of spectra photographed, a very large number of peculiar spectra were found by careful examination of the photographs. . . . By means of bright lines or other spectral peculiarities a large number of novae, variable stars, and other special objects were discovered. The classification and discussion of these objects was carried on chiefly by Mrs. Fleming, under the direction of Pickering.

Mina Fleming's keen vision and her instinct for the unlikely lent themselves admirably to the detection of "novae, variable stars, and other special objects." Novae—those stars that flare, then fade out of sight—and variables—stars of varying intensity—were stellar phenomena that before the age of celestial photography could not have been known or whose existence could only have been conjectured. Now, with scientific detachment, Fleming began to report discoveries of these phenomena with increasing frequency.

Evaluation of many of these discoveries was subject to the prejudice of a community of scientists who found it hard to put credence in anything resulting from methodology so different from traditional practice. Some astronomers actually disclaimed her discoveries, attributing the spectra to flaws on the film. But she was convinced of the integrity of her claims and she had the courage of her convictions.

In 1893 she was invited to speak before the Congress of Astronomy and Astrophysics at the Columbian Exposition at Chicago. In a speech delivered in her rich Scottish accent, she touched on this encrusted prejudice against the work being done at Harvard, not because it diminished her, but because it threatened the integrity of the man to whom she was so intensely loyal. Her argument was a convincing one:

> Photography as applied to astronomy is one of the greatest advances which has been made in this oldest of sciences. . . . you have, ready to your hand and for immediate use, the material for which a visual observer might have to wait for years and certainly for months. This material must also be considered more reliable, for in the case of the visual observer, you have simply his statement of how the object appeared at a given time as seen by him alone, while here you have a photograph in which every star speaks for itself, and which can at any time, now or in the years to come, be compared with any other photographs of the same part of the sky.

Ample proof of the value of such a record came when a European astronomer announced the discovery of a new star. By studying the star's different spectra as shown on plates in her library taken at 8 different times, Fleming determined its life history. The discovering astonomer had observed his star once; Fleming had ferreted out a record of the body that could be read over several years.

But the plates that carried the star's story would have had no value, had they not been so cataloged and so stored as to be immediately available. Mina Fleming's development and refinement of a cataloging system that made possible the fullest utilization of photographic plates was, perhaps, her greatest contribution to astronomy.

Through her diligence she convinced scientists to trust this new method of observation, to believe that the eye of the camera was, in the last analysis, more reliable than the eye of a visual observer.

By demonstrating that skilled use of photographic plates could make classifying and charting the history of stellar bodies a far more objective task, she did much to move astronomy into the realm of hard science. This was perhaps her major contribution to her field, though she was far more widely remembered for her more news-worthy achievements—the finding of new stars.

At that task she was undisputed master. In 1907 she published the "Photographic Study of Variable Stars" in which she listed 222 vari-able stars that she had discovered in the course of her work with the Harvard photographic library. Not content with simply listing these newly identified stars, she had undertaken the very laborious work of measuring the position and the magnitude of sequences of com-parison stars for each of the 222 she had discovered. H. H. Turner, professor of astronomy at Oxford University, wrote of his amaze-ment at the work:

> Many astronomers are deservedly proud to have discovered one variable and content to leave arrangements for its observations to others; the discovery of 222, and the care of their future on this scale, is an achievement bordering on the marvelous.

Despite her record of discovery, Mina Fleming was no glory-seeker relishing the announcements and the limelight. The discov-eries were announced quietly and with thorough documentation.

For Mina Fleming was a modest woman, unassuming and ready always to share her tremendous breadth of knowledge with anyone. She was an administrator who evoked awe and respect, but she was fair-minded; she readily assigned credit to others and wore her honors easily. In those characteristics she was an image of the man who fostered her career.

In the early years, as was the custom, Fleming's work was pub-lished under the name of the director of the observatory. Then, in time, another name began to appear with Pickering's on reports in scientific journals, and eventually, in a show not only of Fleming's status within the observatory but of the magnanimity of the director of the observatory, brief reports of astounding discoveries began to appear over the single name, "M. Fleming."

Thus Mina Fleming became duly recognized as one of the leading astronomers of her day. And she was accorded honors befitting her accomplishments. In 1898 the Harvard Corporation, the board of directors of Harvard University, in recognition of an already accomplished fact, conferred on her the title of Curator of Astronomical Photographs. It was the first official appointment ever accorded a woman by Harvard University.

She was an enthusiastic charter member of the American Astronomical and Astrophysical Society. In 1906 she became the fifth woman, and the first American woman, to be admitted to membership, albeit honorary, in the Royal Astronomical Society of England. The Societe Astronomique de France granted her membership, and the Sociedad Astronomica de Mexico not only gave her honorary membership but also bestowed upon her its Guadalupe Almendaro medal. Wellesley College gave her an honorary appointment, making her a lifetime Fellow of the College.

The honors never diverted her attention or her energy from the tasks at hand. Day by day, year by year, with magnifying eyepiece in hand, she directed astronomical research, painstakingly charted and cross-referenced all manner of new stars, and wrote papers. She also did a vast amount of work in editing the annals, circulars, and other papers produced by the Harvard College Observatory.

An indefatigable worker, she took little time off. Her rare holidays were seized most frequently during the fall of the year when she indulged her great passion for the sport of American football. As energetically as ever she gave herself to the work of the Harvard Observatory, she gave herself to the encouragement of the Harvard Crimson on a Saturday afternoon.

Though she was devoted to her work, her interests were by no means confined to the bounds of the observatory. She raised her son proudly and in 1901 watched him receive a degree in engineering from Massachusetts Institute of Technology. She took joy in her home and her garden, and visiting astronomers were frequently invited to her place close by the observatory to be served an excellent meal of which she was justifiably proud. She was also an expert with the needle, and her Scottish dolls, dressed in exquisitely sewn authentic Highlanders' outfits, were the feature of many fund-raising bazaars around Boston and Cambridge.

All-out participation in all aspects of life characterized Mina Fleming, and her vitality was an inspiration to all who knew her. She seemed larger than life, and when stomach cancer was discovered, it stunned her associates, for they considered this doughty woman indestructible and her presence indispensable. The diagnosis, even several surgeries that followed, failed to slow Fleming. She continued apace, engrossed in the work at hand.

In the fall of 1910 she took a cross-country trip by rail to represent Harvard Observatory at the Union for Solar Research at Mount Wilson in California. On the way home she stopped in Salt Lake City briefly to visit with her son, who was employed there as a mining engineer.

On her return from that trip her great natural vitality seemed to flag. But not her courage. She continued to direct the work of the Draper Memorial, gathering data and dispensing opinions, opinions that sometimes shattered presuppositions and led to discoveries such as the one she shared that morning with Pickering and Russell. Twice in October of 1910 the *New York Times* carried front-page announcements of the discovery of a new star by "Mrs. Williamina Fleming of the Harvard College observatory." The following spring she became critically ill. She was hospitalized in May, developed pneumonia, and succumbed on May 21, 1911, at the age of 54.

At the time of her death the Harvard Observatory library held over 200,000 plates, and she was familiar with every one of them. Edward Pickering saw to the posthumous publication of her last great work, "Stars Having Peculiar Spectra." Listed therein were the 28 new stars—novae—observed during the last quarter century; 10 of them had been Mina Fleming's discovery. It also listed 107 so-called Wolf-Rayet stars, members of a group known by their highly ionized atmospheres. Of those 107, Fleming had herself discovered

94. She had discovered over 300 variable stars; she had recorded 91 meteor trails and 4 meteor spectra. She had determined the composition of all the brighter stars, numbered by hundreds of thousands, and had prepared lists of several thousand that showed peculiarities.

But her accomplishments cannot be adequately cited in a straightforward recital of unparalleled discovery. As Professor Pickering wrote of her in a 1911 testimonial printed in the *Harvard Graduate Magazine*, "She attained remarkable skill in several directions. . . . [She] formed a striking example of a woman who attained success in the higher paths of science. . . ."

Mina Fleming's success could be measured in another way. She made for herself a formidable reputation in a field that was the special province of men. The opportunity for accomplishment in that field came because of Professor Pickering's unusual sensitivity to the talents of women and his determination to provide ample opportunity for the use of such talents. But Mina Fleming's stature must ultimately be attributed to her own intelligence and industry. With characteristic modesty, she herself pointed out that if she was successful it was because astronomy was a field peculiarly suited to women.

In 1893, when she had addressed the Congress of Astronomy and Astrophysics in Chicago, though she had touched on many subjects close to her, she had titled her speech "A Field for Woman's Work," and she addressed the opportunities that lay open to women in astronomy. Here, as in no other field, she foresaw new vistas for women willing to put their talents to work.

"Labor honestly, conscientiously, and steadily," she said, addressing her words to the women in her audience, "and success must crown your efforts." In a phrase she had captured the spirit of her own life.

·~· *Orie Latham Hatcher* ·~·
Altering Attitudes

*A*s Orie Latham Hatcher left her apartment and walked along
the tree-lined streets of Richmond, Virginia, on a late May
morning in 1923, her spirits drooped as visibly as the silk flowers on
her broad-brimmed spring hat. She had opened the New York
Times at breakfast, anticipating some further notice of the fund-
raising activities being carried out by the newly formed New York
City branch of the Southern Woman's Educational Alliance.

Instead, she had come upon an article that quoted, in part, an
editorial written by an angry newspaperman in Jackson, Mississippi.
The editorial, written in reaction to a Times article describing an
SWEA meeting at the Vanderbilt Hotel, avowed that Southerners
were "getting dog-goned tired of being exploited as objects of charity . . . for the amusement of the idle rich in the north who do not
know what to do with their money." The Mississippi editor re-

minded his readers that the mothers and grandmothers of Southern women "were being educated in splendid ante-bellum colleges when the mothers and grandmothers of some who seek to patronize us were taking in washing for a living." His remarks would have been almost laughable, had Hatcher not known how deadly serious he must have been.

Disheartened by this fresh reminder of the difficulties that had plagued her efforts from the start, Hatcher asked herself once more why she'd ever dreamed she could change attitudes that seemed to be graven in stone. Southern women didn't want change—they wanted only their comfortable homes, their glorified memories of days gone by.

Despite her inner turmoil, Hatcher's spirits lifted at the sight of the familiar burst of color that greeted her on Mrs. Lofton's corner —white azaleas in full bloom, pinks just beginning to fade. To her surprise, she saw the lady of the house standing near the back gate.

"Good morning, Miss Hatcher," she called cheerfully. "Would you like these azaleas for your office?"

Puzzled by this unexpected gesture from one of Richmond's wealthiest and most influential citizens, and amazed that this ultra-conservative woman even recognized her, Hatcher accepted the proffered bouquet with a murmured, "How thoughtful."

"It's nothing, really," the older woman answered. "I've intended to offer you flowers before now. You see," she ventured, "I watch you walking to work every morning and, to tell the truth, I envy you because you always look as if you have to get where you're going."

As Orie Hatcher moved onto Grace Street and into the Women's Professional Building, there was renewed vigor in her step. "Yes, Mrs. Lofton," she said aloud as she opened her office door, "I do have to get where I'm going—so that your daughters and grand-daughters won't have to sit in their breakfast rooms and envy women who have somewhere to go."

With a vase of azaleas brightening her desk, she reached for pen and paper and began at once a letter informing the Mississippi editor that, far from being "a Northern institute propelled by missionary zeal to educate the benighted South," the Southern Woman's

Educational Alliance was as Southern in its origins and as honorable in its intentions as the United Daughters of the Confederacy.

As SWEA's founder and president, Orie Latham Hatcher knew whereof she spoke. Her father's family had been respected residents of Virginia since leaving England several generations earlier, and William Eldridge Hatcher himself was a leader among Southern Baptist ministers. Her mother, Oranie Virginia Snead Hatcher, was a spirited and intelligent young woman brought up in the company of 5 brothers, all of whom served in the Confederate Army. Virginia Snead herself attended Fluvana Institute, where her senior thesis proclaimed that "if women could not do as they chose, they might [at least] think as they chose and get ready for action."

This remarkable young woman saw in W.E. Hatcher a lively spirit akin to her own, and in 1864, near the close of the Civil War, the two were married. Their third child and second daughter, Orie Latham, was born December 19, 1868, in Petersburg, Virginia. Of the 6 additional children who came afterward, 3 daughters lived to maturity.

In 1875, when Orie was 7, the family moved to Richmond, where Dr. Hatcher began what was to be a 26-year term as pastor of Grace Street Baptist Church. Both parents showed single-minded devotion to the work of the church and to the imperatives of mission efforts at home and abroad, an example that was not lost on young Orie. In later years, she recalled that she "belonged to the sort of family . . . that always had to be meeting some sort of imperative outside claims that would have their arduous way," and her own life continued that pattern.

Orie idolized her father and sought his company at every opportunity. Believing that the gospel called for social action, he spent his weekdays acting upon the principles he preached every Sunday. His success in cleaning up slums in a cotton-mill town, providing clothes and shoes for poor children in Richmond, and establishing an academy where boys and girls could reach their full potential made him somewhat of a legend in his time.

Mrs. Hatcher's major interest lay in foreign missions, and the

Hatcher children gained their earliest understanding of geography from the stories told by missionaries who had lived in faraway places. Fund-raising efforts for home and foreign mission projects were common activities, and young Orie quickly learned that where the needs of others were concerned, there need be no hesitancy in asking for financial assistance.

In 1883, at age 15, Orie Hatcher became Richmond Female Institute's youngest graduate, and for the next 2 years she taught school in Richmond. At this point a wealthy Northerner, a friend of Dr. Hatcher, came to visit the family. Impressed by Orie's bright mind and quick wit, he offered to send her to Vassar. The proposal created considerable shock waves, with one Richmond citizen telling Dr. Hatcher that he'd rather see his daughter in hell than send her to a Yankee college. "Well," the minister is said to have replied, "you send yours to Hell; mine's going to Vassar."

Accustomed to being at the head of her class, Orie was shocked and surprised to find herself far behind her Vassar classmates, and she found little comfort in her teachers' assurances that this situation was inevitable—Southern girls, due to their weaker academic backgrounds, were always behind at first. Having caught up to her class, she graduated from Vassar in 1888, at the age of 20, and took a teaching job at Miss Belle Peer's school in Louisville, Kentucky. In 1892 she left Kentucky to join the faculty of Richmond Female Institute, determined to do what she could to increase the intellectual challenge offered to students at her alma mater.

During her teaching years in Richmond, Hatcher spent a summer in Europe. The highlight of that trip was a visit to Geneva, where she spent happy hours in the company of a young American, a Princeton graduate studying philosophy in Germany. The intellectual stimulation of their intense conversations on religion and literature stood in sharp contrast to the conversations she had known in Richmond. Here was a man who could challenge her assumptions, stretch her mind, make her feel alive again.

Though they were in all ways compatible, Orie Hatcher wrote in her travel diary that she never saw the young scholar "in the light of a possible lover. . . . Indeed, from the first he appeared as quite impossible, for I had not the vanity to think that I might ensnare one that was handsome as a dream." The young man's own feelings on this matter remain a mystery, but it is known that Hatcher was so convinced of her own homeliness that she would likely have had difficulty believing that any man could find her physically attractive.

From early childhood, she had been convinced of her plainness, seeing nothing remarkable in her blue eyes, brown hair, and decidedly ordinary complexion. In several instances, she scratched her own face out of family, school, and newspaper photographs. She assiduously avoided looking at herself in mirrors, taking along her eldest niece to serve as model when she shopped for hats. Yet, even as she winced to see the reflection of a face that could never earn her the title "Southern belle," she took comfort in the realization that her mind had a beauty that could intrigue and even dazzle. And she learned early on to cultivate her intellectual beauty, looking always toward a career as scholar rather than as wife.

She evaluated her experiences in Europe in light of her goals as scholar and saw at once that her intellectual growth was severely limited by her life in Richmond. The stimulation she needed could not be found in the easy-going atmosphere of her native South. She had been intellectually challenged at Vassar, and she now sought still further challenge by enrolling in the PhD program at the University of Chicago. In 1903 she received her doctorate in English literature, and her dissertation, "John Fletcher: A Study in Dramatic Method," was published in 1905.

With this portion of her goal accomplished, she chose to stay North, accepting a part-time position as reader in the English department at Bryn Mawr, one of the most prestigious women's colleges in the nation. Though she quickly became a respected member of the faculty, she sensed that she was being kept on the fringe of academic life at Bryn Mawr, and she believed that young Southern women who came to the school as students felt the same ostracism.

Remembering her own undergraduate experience at Vassar, she was again made painfully aware of the fact that few Southern women were well enough prepared academically to fall comfortably into the flow of life at schools like Bryn Mawr. In 1906, convinced of the universally poor academic background of Southern women, she helped to organize the Virginia Association of Colleges and Schools for Girls, a group whose chief purpose was to set standards for the schools and thereby improve the quality of educational programs for Southern women.

By 1908, Hatcher had become a lecturer, by 1910 an associate professor, and soon thereafter the founder of Bryn Mawr's Department of Comparative Literature. Orie Hatcher had clearly risen above the handicap of her own weak academic beginnings, but her contentment was disturbed by thoughts of women at home in Virginia, women destined to spend their lives as she felt her mother had spent hers—running the home and tending the family so that their husbands could pursue their chosen careers.

Her earlier efforts had raised the standards of Virginia's colleges for women, but she now saw that raising standards wasn't enough. Southern women could not profit from such improvements unless they were first made aware of the educational and vocational opportunities available to them, then made to see that these options were valid as well as viable ones.

The task was a formidable one, for most Southerners saw no need for women to pursue occupations outside the home unless financial considerations forced them to do so. As matters stood, few women gave serious thought to pursuing a career outside that of homemaker. For those women who did work, Southern society set strict conditions. Teaching had always been considered an honorable occupation, if one absolutely had to work. In recent years, social work, library work, and nursing had gained acceptance as proper occupations for women. And though there were those who still had reservations concerning women's employment in offices, clerical work was fast becoming a predominantly female field.

But Orie Hatcher wanted more. She wanted women to be able to go beyond those limits, to pursue careers in medicine, law, institutional management, dentistry, landscape architecture—in any area they chose. She knew that Boston, New York, and Philadelphia boasted newly founded bureaus of occupation, or appointment bureaus, for trained women, but no such organizations had been formed in the South—perhaps because there were so few highly trained women looking for employment in the South. In the South there was simply no interest in the work of women—not even among women themselves. As an observer of the scene had noted some years before,

> [T]he average woman of the South . . . is satisfied with her condition. She loves her church and believes in her preacher. She is Pauline in her ideas and therefore loves the music of her chains. . . . Chivalry has allotted her sphere, and her soul has been so pressed by social and ecclesiastical rigidity that . . . [she] does not transgress the limits.

Combating this well-entrenched attitude was seen as the major challenge facing the group of women that Orie Latham Hatcher called together in May of 1914. Meeting in the home of Mary Cooke Branch Munford, a leader of the Coordinate College League then fighting to establish a college for women on the University of Virginia's exclusively male campus, this small group of determined women discussed the currently available educational and vocational opportunities for women in Virginia. Then, convinced of the need for increasing those opportunities, they established that day the organization that was soon to be the Virginia Bureau of Vocations for Women. Determined to help girls and women in the South "meet the changing conditions confronting women in modern life," the group set out "to counteract the tradition that any educated woman who must earn her living must choose between teaching and stenography and to show her that there are really hundreds of other possibilities from which to choose."

Hatcher had picked with great care the women who would help her to bring her dream into reality. She knew that the support of prominent, well-educated women would give the Virginia bureau a status, credence, and legitimacy that it would not otherwise have had, and she knew that their reactions to her plans and tactics would give her an early indication of the reactions she could expect from other Southerners of their social standing. She also counted on the women within the group she assembled to influence the membership of other civic or women's groups, thus building for her program a network of supporters that stretched far beyond her own personal sphere of influence.

By October of 1914, the fledgling Virginia Bureau of Vocations for Women opened an office in the Richmond YWCA building on Fifth Street, and promotional material was prepared and distributed. Hatcher herself was again at Bryn Mawr, but in the spring of that academic year, at age 47, she decided to give up her teaching career and devote herself full-time to expanding the educational and vocational opportunities of Southern women.

Having been away for more than a decade, Dr. Orie Latham Hatcher returned to Richmond as a virtual unknown. Though her earlier attempts to raise the standards of Virginia's schools for women and girls had given her limited visibility with educators in the state, she knew that the growth of the bureau depended upon establishing a much wider support base. She needed, also, to convince the people of Virginia of her abilities as an organizer, to show them that they could trust her leadership.

For years she had been at work on *A Book for Shakespeare Plays and Pageants*, a volume designed to give school, community, and professional groups the necessary background for presenting the works of William Shakespeare. She had timed publication for 1916, the three hundredth anniversary of Shakespeare's death, and she now realized that the bureau could gain almost instant recognition through the sponsorship of a major celebration of that anniversary.

As president of the bureau, Orie Hatcher served as overall coordinator of Richmond's Shakespearean festival. In constant contact with the hundreds involved in the affair, she had ample opportunity to show her organizational skills to great advantage. By early spring, the *Richmond Times-Dispatch* noted that "fashionable society these days talks of little else than the big Shakespeare pageant and the members of the smart set who are to take part in it." With more than 2,000 citizens of Richmond involved in its production and over 8,000 others enjoying the drama, dance, and music, the Shakespeare pageant was an overwhelming success in every way.

As predicted, the pageant heightened local curiosity concerning the work of the bureau, but it did little to foster any real understanding of that work. Orie Hatcher had brought home to Richmond ideas totally foreign to Southerners. Only after having lived and studied outside the South had she herself embraced the values she was now attempting to impart to people who had never given much thought to the idea of women having, or even wanting to have, a career other than that of homemaker.

While the women's vocational bureaus of New York, Philadelphia, and Boston had been organized because educated women felt they needed help in obtaining professional positions, the Virginia bureau had been formed because Orie Hatcher realized that Southern women needed encouragement even to aspire to professional positions. There was, then, no unrest, no spirit of revolution, only "a half realized idea . . . that in [the] social and political organism there is something out of gear."

In an attempt to find out just what was out of gear, Hatcher and her bureau began research into the status of women as professionals in Virginia. Though 1910 census figures showed a female population of 1,026,000, bureau researchers located only 12,000 women engaged in professional work. Most of these were teachers, nurses, and musicians; women practitioners in professions such as law or medicine were so rare as to be cause for much attention, often of a negative nature.

These statistics should not have been surprising, in view of the limited educational opportunities open to women in Virginia. Despite the continued boasting of proud Southerners who praised the "splendid ante-bellum colleges" available to their women, as of 1916 most of the schools designed especially for women students turned out homemakers, not scholars. While most Southerners saw nothing wrong with this sort of education, Orie Hatcher insisted that "no woman of normal mentality is adequately educated today unless she has enough general education to lay broad, strong foundations and, in addition, training for doing competently some wisely chosen type of work."

Being realistic, Hatcher saw that acceptance of women into graduate and professional schools within the state of Virginia was likely to be a long time in coming, and she turned her attention in 1916 to a project of more immediate promise—the development of better educational opportunities for women in fields in which they were already accepted, notably social work, public health, and stenography.

She helped to found the Richmond School of Social Work and Public Health, designing a program that gave students rudimentary training in public health and/or social work, training that would qualify them for immediate employment in these areas, as well as for admission to more highly specialized programs offered by schools outside the South. By giving women who might otherwise have remained on the volunteer side of health care and social work the opportunity for professional training, the new school helped them become skilled professionals capable of making sizable contributions within their chosen fields.

In similar fashion, the bureau sought to give women interested in secretarial work enough training to enable them to make significant advances in the business and professional world. Seeing secretarial work not as an end in itself but as "an invaluable entering wedge to many interesting types of executive and other work," Hatcher was dismayed to find that most business schools throughout the South offered courses designed to enable a woman to serve as typist or filing clerk or bookkeeper, but not to help her rise to more responsible work within an organization.

To combat this trend, she helped design a program for what was to become Smithdeal Secretarial School of Richmond. Founded to "equip women for responsible secretarial work and to raise the calling [of secretary] to the professional standing which it is assuming in so many other parts of the country," the school served as a model for the subsequent development of secretarial programs in the South.

Many Southerners who supported the idea of training women as secretaries opposed any move toward training them as professionals, insisting that such training made a woman less "womanly." To dispel such fears, Hatcher organized a 1918 conference of business and professional women, choosing as speakers women who had grown up in the South but who now held professional positions elsewhere.

Though trained in business, journalism, law, medicine, and public health, these women had all retained the manners and the magnetism that Hatcher knew would be attractive to conservative Southerners.

In her opening remarks at the conference, she praised the speakers for "achieving distinguished success in traditionally masculine callings and yet keeping all the social graces upon which Virginia so fervently insists." While such remarks would seem far too conciliatory for use in the world of the late twentieth century, in the Virginia of 1918 they served well, and the assembled speakers were summarily acknowledged as exemplary role models for the young women of the state, models that proved beyond a doubt that femininity need not be sacrificed to careers.

There were significant psychological benefits in another move made by the bureau during that same year—the opening of the Women's Professional Building, a structure offering both office space and living quarters to the business and professional women of Richmond. Although the establishment of a Women's Professional Building in a city with so few women professionals gave a sense of solidarity to the city's career-minded women, the existence of such a building was of little help to those women who found their entry into the professions hampered by lack of educational opportunities within the state. As of 1918, the year the building was opened, all graduate and professional programs within the state of Virginia were still closed to women.

In an effort to break down the barriers posed by such discrimination, the bureau engaged Dr. Margaret P. Kuyk, a Richmond physician, for a series of lectures on "Medicine as a Career for Women." Under continual pressure from Hatcher, Kuyk, and others, the Medical College of Virginia agreed to begin a program for women, and the bureau set about publicizing this new opportunity and recruiting students. Within 6 weeks, 18 qualified women had enrolled, and Virginia women were at last free to study medicine within their home state.

One by one, other barriers were broken, and by 1920 women could also study law, pharmacy, dentistry, business administration, public health, and social work in Virginia schools. The bureau had been a prime mover in bringing about these changes, and Hatcher had already begun to exhibit what one reporter later described as "a fantastic capacity for making people do things they did not expect to do."

However, faced with an annual budget of less than $2500, Hatcher knew that continued progress depended upon enlarging the scope of the program. From the beginning, the impact of her efforts and those of the Virginia Bureau of Occupations for Women had stretched far beyond Virginia, and the organization's goals had always been broader than its name suggested. Now, as a first step toward establishing a support base outside the state, she dropped "Virginia" from the bureau's name. Then, in early 1921, the bureau became the Southern Woman's Educational Alliance (SWEA), and Hatcher gained the broad constituency she had so long sought. Under its new name, SWEA invited the interest and support of Southern women living or working outside the region, women who would be sympathetic to the cause because they had seen for themselves the vast difference in educational and vocational opportunities within and without the South.

Describing the alliance as "a bridge between the Southern girl and the right opportunity," Hatcher traveled to New York City to meet with leaders in social work, vocational bureaus, and universities and to enlist their financial and moral support for the work of the bureau. She invited the deans of such prestigious institutions as Vassar and Smith to become board members, thereby ensuring their support for the program and their interest in providing scholarship aid for girls recommended by the bureau.

Encouraged by the enthusiastic response of her new constituency, Hatcher enlarged her goals. The alliance would explore and analyze the current and potential educational, vocational, and economic status of women in the South, then dispense the accumulated data through conferences, programs, and publications. In addition, SWEA would continue to work for expanding opportunities for educational and professional training within the Southern states and for scholarships and loans for Southern girls of ability and ambition who wished to attend schools outside the South.

No longer limited to $1000 dreams, Hatcher boldly announced a campaign to raise $100,000 as a first step toward reaching alliance goals. In mounting that campaign, she called upon all the fund-raising and publicity methods she had seen her parents employ during her childhood years. She formed a New York City branch of SWEA and gained the support and public endorsement of such figures as Irene Langhorne Gibson, wife of artist Charles Dana Gibson and a model for his famous "Gibson Girl."

Hatcher urged Mrs. Gibson and other branch members to make promotion of alliance activities a part of every social organization to which they belonged, and New York City's Southern elite responded with a flurry of fund-raising events, most of them well-publicized social and cultural affairs. It was the *New York Times* account of a 1923 New York branch fund-raising drive aimed at helping SWEA to "popularize higher education among Southern women" that so ired the Mississippi newspaper editor.

By the end of 1924, $31,000 had been raised by the New York branch. Art shows and music recitals in Greenwich Village, gala balls and teas in Manhattan, and annual benefit performances by the New York Metropolitan Opera continued to bring in funds for alliance work. In addition, monies were garnered from SWEA branches in Chicago, Atlanta, and Washington, D.C., and from various philanthropic foundations.

With this new financial support, Hatcher was able to increase her program for guidance in the colleges. She began with research aimed at determining what needs there were for occupational guidance in Southern colleges. Having identified those needs, Hatcher moved to meet them. She developed a speaker's bureau of professional women who, for a nominal fee, appeared at member schools. Her speakers challenged their listeners, as well as informed them, and stressed the almost unlimited potential that could be tapped in women, once "all the power folded within [them] could be released."

The alliance then sent out letters urging heads of Southern colleges to establish programs of vocational guidance, and reactions to those letters were indicative of the status of vocational guidance in those institutions. The president of Agnes Scott, a private women's college in Decatur, Georgia, replied that Agnes Scott College was dedicated to the proposition that homemaker "was the greatest vocation in the world for women" and that the college had no intention of introducing any other vocational subject. A spokesman for Baylor, a Texas Baptist college, replied that "the matter [of vocational guidance] is so new to me that I am unable to make any suggestions that would be helpful."

To alter these attitudes, the alliance organized a vocational guidance conference, inviting school officials from elementary and secondary schools and representatives from women's clubs and the YWCA. In the keynote address, Hatcher defined vocational guidance as "helping people to find the right calling, to prepare for it, and to succeed in it." She emphasized the importance of offering such guidance to children in the lower grades as well as to college students, and she stressed the fact that vocational guidance for boys as well as for girls could solve problems in juvenile delinquency and unemployment.

This conference whetted interest in vocational guidance programs, and the alliance called upon Dr. Iva Peters of Goucher College, one of the country's foremost guidance experts, to devise a model course in vocational guidance and set that course in motion on a few select college campuses. Peters and SWEA staff members joined with college personnel in presenting this course on the social and economic history of women and the occupational fields currently open to them.

Branch fund-raising efforts soon made other alliance research projects financially feasible. Well-qualified young women were hired to conduct studies on such topics as scholarships and fellowships available in Southern colleges, opportunities for the educated blind, incentives in various fields of employment, activities of alumnae associations, and many other aspects of educational and vocational development in the South.

Several of these studies became a part of *Occupations for Women,* a 1927 publication that Hatcher called the alliance's "definitive contribution to occupational information." On the basis of an extensive survey of employment opportunities in Atlanta, a progressive Southern city, and Richmond, a conservative one, the book presented an overview of the number of women active in various fields and the salaries they were earning in those fields. In addition, the volume described in detail each vocational field listed, including the education and training prerequisite for success therein and the psychological and other nonfinancial advantages and disadvantages of pursuing a career in that field.

The book was divided into three main categories that were established according to prevailing popular opinion as to the types of jobs that were suitable for men and for women: (1) jobs that the public tended to see as suited to women (i.e., nursing and the teaching of children); (2) jobs that were usually seen as suited to both men and women (i.e., creative arts, social work); and (3) jobs that were generally considered suitable only for men (i.e., medicine, law, engineering).

But those arbitrary divisions were not quite so clear-cut as they seemed. Within category 2, the category containing jobs considered suitable for women as well as men, Hatcher detected a significant subzone of activity. Males entered this subzone "only to decide what ha[d] to be done," leaving all the real work therein to women. To those women, "by the working of an apparently unswerving instinct," fell all routine and mechanical tasks, all tasks requiring little or no initiative. Thus, while women were not actually barred from the fields in category 2, most of them remained confined to this less-than-professional subzone, a zone Hatcher saw as "down below the level where the business or profession as such [actually] begins. . . ."

A *New York Times* review praised *Occupations for Women* for casting light "on a region formerly dark, even to itself" and noted that the book indicates that the daughters of the "dreary, bemuffled, indolent lady" formerly associated with the South have "become vocal, not in a violent way, but with a clear, quiet tone that assumes their positions in the modern active world."

Practical and commonsensical as it was, *Occupations for Women* was, for its day, a radical work. The basic assumption behind the book—that women should and could consider entering any career they wished—was radical to many Americans, and particularly to Southerners. Yet, as one reviewer noted, "the entire book has been conceived in a manner for which the word dignity is the only one suitable."

While the research for *Occupations for Women* was underway, Orie Hatcher had become increasingly concerned about the rural girls who were migrating to urban centers of the South. Often these girls left school early in search of city jobs for which they were ill-equipped. In 1924 Hatcher had proposed a 4-year program of study of rural educational needs. That study featured experimentation with various types of guidance concepts and culminated in the publication of 2 significant reports.

In 1926, Hatcher had made a tour of 23 mountain schools in 4 states and agreed to help Konnarock Training School in Smyth County, Virginia, develop an educational program for the Kentucky, North Carolina, Tennessee, West Virginia, and Virginia youth in attendance there. A 3-year study of the school included a study of the community as well, plus an extensive analysis of 38 female students, ages 7 to 17. From this research came *A Mountain School* (1930) and *Guiding Rural Boys and Girls* (1930).

Convinced that a rural school such as Konnarock could and should find ways to make its educational program relevant to the life a child would lead after leaving school, Hatcher proposed that rural schools should provide a dual course of study. One course would be especially designed for those students who were exceptionally bright and who wished to attend college or to obtain work in the city, while the other would cater to those students who planned to stay home and farm.

Such innovative thinking drew the attention of the National Vocational Guidance Association, and SWEA was asked to establish a rural division for that group. Indeed, during the 1930s most SWEA activities were given over to vocational guidance for rural youth. The organization sponsored several conferences and institutes on rural educational development, in-service guidance programs, health care, and the problems of urban migration.

In 1930 the alliance published *Rural Girls in the City for Work*, a study revealing the employment, salary, and living conditions of 250 rural girls who had left their homes for work in Durham, North Carolina, and Richmond, Virginia. The book sparked investigation into the lives of girls who left Northern rural communities for New York City and other large metropolitan areas. To provide shelter and advice to young people from rural areas who had come to the city for work, branch offices of the alliance then set up youth migration institutes in New York City and Washington, D.C., as well as in Richmond, Virginia, and Durham, North Carolina.

In 1932 Hatcher's views on guidance for rural youth were included in a vocational guidance volume issued by the White House Conference on Child Health and Protection. As in all her past projects, Hatcher increased her base of support for the work with rural youth by enlisting the aid of influential people and powerful organizations. Eleanor Roosevelt became a patron for fund-raising efforts and acted as hostess of a 1934 alliance-sponsored meeting at the White House. Four years later, she and Orie Latham Hatcher discussed "What's Ahead for Rural Young People" on a national radio broadcast, and Roosevelt often praised SWEA activities in her speeches and newspaper interviews.

By 1937, Hatcher was looking to even broader horizons, and she explained to the executive board members of the alliance that "a sectional name is a handicap in any effort to get money" and that the name Southern Woman's Educational Alliance no longer described either the work or the scope of their organization. In one final evolution, SWEA became the Alliance for Guidance of Rural Youth, the name it retained until its dissolution in 1963.

From the beginning Hatcher had run the organization almost single-handedly, though she had relied on the publicity and funds supplied by various branch offices. To meet the exigencies brought by the depression years of the 1930s, she had made staff cuts, closed the Atlanta office, and moved alliance headquarters into an extra room in her apartment. Yet she had managed to keep the organization going. Hatcher herself was well and strong, even into her seventies. From 1940 to 1944 she took an active part in the activities of the White House Conference on Children in a Democracy.

Then, in late March of 1946, with her bags packed and her white gloves hanging freshly washed and ready to be donned for an early morning trip to Washington, D.C., Orie Latham Hatcher suffered a cerebral hemorrhage. She contracted pneumonia soon thereafter and died on April 1, 1946, at the age of 77.

Her funeral, held in the library of her Gresham Court apartment, was conducted by Glynn Morris, a young man from Appalachia whose potential she had noted on one of her visits to mountain schools and whose oration gave testimony to the influence for good that she had exerted in his life and the lives of countless others down through the years. Armed with a first-hand knowledge of the manners and mores of the people she sought to influence, Orie Latham Hatcher had brought about changes that would have been staunchly resisted, had they been introduced by an outsider unfamiliar with the social, religious, and political milieu of the South.

Her burial at Richmond's Hollywood Cemetery effectively signaled the end of such changes, for though the alliance survived her by 17 years, it was never again a vital force. Perhaps it had simply outlived its usefulness, for Hatcher herself had said she did not expect the work to continue indefinitely. Perhaps, as some have said, her strength and spirit had so dominated the movement that her death left her followers without the direction and leadership needed to continue the work.

But even if, as one biographer has insisted, the Southern Woman's Educational Alliance was but the lengthened shadow of Orie Latham Hatcher, there is no doubt that the influence of that shadow is felt, even today, through the thousands of men and women whose lives were brightened and whose opportunities were broadened by her untiring efforts on their behalf.

⁓ *Leta Stetter Hollingworth* ⁓
An Experimental Life

*A*s *she cleared the breakfast table, Leta Stetter Hollingworth thought back over the morning's conversation. What had triggered it all? Was it Harry's mention of the upcoming seminar in Boston? Or could it have been the offhand manner in which he asked about her plans for the day?*

No matter. The important thing was that on this crisp autumn morning she had finally been able to air frustrations she'd endured in silence for nearly two years, frustrations she hadn't really been able to verbalize before, even to herself.

After all, it seemed so selfish to complain. She had everything a woman could want—marriage to a well-thought-of university instructor; a small but cozy apartment in Columbia Heights; long, uninterrupted days in which to perform her household duties; and leisurely evenings in which to hear her husband's accounts of his latest plans and accomplishments.

To most women of 1910, hers was a storybook world, a world that should have given her complete satisfaction. In reality, it was a world whose restrictions had pushed her to the breaking point. But now, after this morning's outburst, now at least Harry knew. He knew that the cooking, the cleaning, the sewing, the washing, and the ironing that filled her days were not enough. And though she had felt guilty to voice such feelings, he even knew that hearing of his numerous professional achievements, far from making her happy, only made her all the more depressed.

"Do you call this a worthwhile life?" she had demanded. "Staying at home and eating a lone pork chop while you're off giving speeches or attending seminars?"

Shocked by her anger and devastated by the tears that followed, he had left home looking dazed and bewildered. Poor man. In her more rational moments, she knew it wasn't all his fault. Though she resented his insensitivity to her frustrations, it was hardly fair to blame him for the situation she found herself in. Who could have predicted that married life would be like this, that the union they'd waited so long for would threaten, rather than enhance, their relationship?

As she wiped the countertop dry and hung the dishcloth on the rack, a sudden thought came to her. There was a basic flaw in her thinking. It wasn't being married that had thwarted her career plans. After all, Harry was married, yet his marriage would not have kept him from teaching in New York City's public schools. Harry was married, yet his marriage would not have lessened his chances for a graduate fellowship. Harry was married, yet he was not burdened by endless, mindless household chores. She had been blaming marriage, but it was not being married that had doomed her to life as a domestic—it was being a married female.

Why had she not seen it this clearly before? Society's message was all too plain: A woman was encouraged to marry and bear children. She might even, in rare instances, be grudgingly permitted to choose a professional career instead of a family. But she must not attempt both.

That was the rule, all right. But where had it come from? How could a society impose such a discriminatory ethic? And why should she accept it? Taking her coat and hat from their rack by the door, she turned her back on the basket of unironed clothes and moved out of the apartment, down the stairs, and into the bright October day. She was bound for the university library, determined to read all the theories, explore all the excuses, understand all the reasons men had given for her restricted status, then use every means within her power to disprove and discredit those theories so that no other young woman need ever find herself trapped by laws and conventions she had had no part in making.

In the autumn of 1910, 24-year-old Leta Stetter Hollingworth could hardly have known how successful her efforts would eventually be. But she was well prepared for her task. Since her childhood she had known that life was not always fair, and she had managed to escape injustice before. The difference now was that in researching her own cause, she would be cracking a mold that had stifled the ambitions of thousands of women.

Born in 1886 in a dugout in the White River area of northwest Nebraska, just south of the Dakota Territory, Leta Anne Stetter was said to be the first white child born in Dawes County. She came from a long line of pioneers, hard-working men and women whose travels read like a historian's account of the settling of the United States. Thankful for this pioneering heritage, she later recalled that her early years on the prairie had given her "a splendid set of work habits and all the benefits to be derived from mastering farm animals, blizzards, sand storms, and cacti."

She saw all these and more on the sandhill homestead in which she spent her early days. Her mother, Margaret Elinor Danley, was a soft-spoken, gentle woman whose years in an Illinois academy had given her a love of Latin and botany, as well as a certain finish, a degree of polish uncommon among prairie women. At 22 Margaret

Danley and her parents had moved to Chadron, Nebraska, where her father, a farmer and an ordained Presbyterian minister, settled in, full of hope and faith in the provident guidance of his God. The following year, 1885, Margaret Danley met and married John G. Stetter, a strongly gregarious young cowboy of German descent, a man whom in-laws later described as "easily weaned from serious pursuits" and always ready to dance a jig, "even in what should have been the most tragic moments of his aimless life."

This high-spirited father was away when his wife gave birth in her parents' small prairie dugout to an 8½-pound girl she named Leta Anne. It took two telegrams to bring the new father home, and once home he expressed his sentiments baldly: "I'd give a thousand dollars if it was a boy." His wife recorded his comment in a tiny leather-bound journal she kept, then added her own: "I would not give her for half a dozen boys."

Papa Stetter's interest in family life remained scant over the next 3 years, though he returned home often enough to father 2 more daughters. Margaret Danley Stetter died on February 9, 1890, the day after the birth of her third daughter. Left with 3 girls, all under the age of 4, John Stetter came home even less often. By now Grandpa and Grandma Danley had moved from their dugout into a sod house, and the 3 little girls settled into life in the Scottish-Irish Presbyterian tradition.

Samuel Danley struggled valiantly to make the dry-land farm produce the crops its meager rainfall and sandy soil could never support. His little granddaughters did their part to help—milking, gathering pumpkins, tending the turkeys and chickens, and pulling the catch on the corn seeder as Grandpa drove the team.

Their toys were the natural objects of the prairie, and their clothes were plain and simple dresses of unbleached linen. Their undergarments were fashioned from old flour sacks, and little Leta started to read by sounding out the syllables of Chadron Roller Mills, the words printed on her underpants. Her more formal education during her early years took place in a one-room log schoolhouse, a learning environment that she later judged as "excellent in every respect," since it featured small classes, all of nature for a laboratory, and individualized instruction.

For this daughter of the prairie, aesthetic pleasures were the ones nature bestowed. Leta was a highly sensitive child, and she later recalled that she cried at the sweetness of birds singing, having no other expression for the emotions that gripped her until she learned "the medium . . . of written words that can make a sunset beam or a flower bloom forever."

A sense of loss pervaded her childhood. There was first the deeply felt loss of a mother whose memory was praised by all who had known her. Then life suddenly took 10-year-old Leta away from the farm and into Chadron, away from the one-room schoolhouse and into the town school. Then still another move took the girls and their grandparents to Colorado. It was a move that Grandpa Danley did not long survive, and it was his death, in 1898, that returned 12-year-old Leta and her 2 sisters to John Stetter's care.

By this time that happy wanderer had been rancher, peddler, trader, teamster, absentee farmer, speculator, and owner of several different bars and entertainment halls. He had moved to Valentine, Nebraska, and he had taken a new wife, a woman whose hostile treatment made Leta's teen years "a fiery furnace." Under her harsh rule, the girls rose at 5:00 each weekday morning to tend to all household chores before school began and rushed home to perform myriad afternoon chores. Saturdays were given over to heavy cleaning and sweeping, and Sundays to baking. Though Grandma Danley, too, now lived in Valentine with her son, the new Mrs. Stetter forbade her to visit the girls. Even daring to speak to the kindly old woman when they met her on the street drew such severe punishment that they began to go out of their way to avoid her, suffering great pangs of guilt for their cowardice.

During those turbulent years, as in later life, the image Leta held of her mother served to sustain and inspire her, for, as she later wrote, "If at any time I do true or worthy things it is and will be because my mother's spirit has had power 'to live again in minds made better.'" Old enough at last to find some relief in written expression of her feelings, she began to write poetry, plaintive, wistful lines that spoke often of loss.

> And the Lone Pine standing patient,
> Where the wild winds wage their strife,
> Beaten and scarred and crippled,
> Like a broken, lonely life,
> Is telling again the story
> As the winds thro' its branches moan,
> Of a soul lifted high o'er its brothers
> That must bear the storm alone.

Leta lived out her teen years as the Lone Pine. She went to school with her brain "in a turmoil" and worked "like the very Dickens for [her] soul's salvation." That salvation lay in graduating from Valentine High with sufficient credits to gain admission to the University of Nebraska at Lincoln, a move that would put over 250 miles of open prairie between her and her stepmother.

In 1902, at age 15, that salvation was accomplished, and she left Valentine behind her and began her college career. Away from the horror of her home life, Leta Stetter blossomed into beautiful young womanhood. She was "small, lithe and graceful . . . full of enthusiasm and animation . . ." with an "inexhaustible interest in human beings." She had a great capacity for fun, but she applied herself studiously. Through 4 years at the university she achieved a brilliant academic record. She was inducted into Phi Beta Kappa, was literary editor of *The Daily Nebraskan*, served on the staffs of 2 other school publications, was elected Poet of the Class of 1906, and graduated with a B.A. in literature and creative writing. Harshly realistic about what it took to be a writer and about the odds against attaining true excellence in the field, she took courses that led to a teaching certificate and embarked upon a high school teaching career designed to enable her to save toward the day when she could marry Harry Levi Hollingworth, a classmate at the University of Nebraska who had gone east for a PhD in psychology from Columbia University in New York.

She and Harry had met during his sophomore year, and they

began dating almost at once, enjoying tennis, bridge, the theater, and long walks in the country, as well as endless discussions of life and the possibilities it offered for those who dared to live it fully. During the 2 long years of their separation, Leta taught in Nebraska and Harry studied in New York. Then on December 31, 1908, in New York City, 22-year-old Leta Stetter became Mrs. Harry Levi Hollingworth. By the following spring, her husband completed his PhD work and accepted an instructorship at Barnard College, Columbia University, a post that paid $1,000 for the academic year.

On this modest budget, Leta Hollingworth's own pursuit of graduate work was an impossible dream, and since her marital status made her ineligible to teach in the city's public schools, she found herself with no meaningful work. When she was finally able to afford a few graduate classes in English literature, she found them to be "dry bones," incapable of holding her interest. She became increasingly restless and frustrated, and only after she recognized the implicit injustice in having to give up her own career in deference to that of her husband was she able to see the cause of her resentment. It was that moment of recognition that freed her to move forward again with real purpose.

Fortunately, once her husband was made aware of her frustrations, he offered support, encouragement, and a sense of direction. He urged her to begin with course work in psychology, a field that seemed especially well-suited to one so determined to analyze and understand her own emotions. She enrolled at Columbia in 1911, taking a course from Professor Edward L. Thorndike, a man well known for his firm belief in the theory that males were more given to genius than females. Hollingworth herself felt sure that any differences between the accomplishments of males and females could be explained by the sociological rather than biological limitations of women, and she took it upon herself to prove her view.

The newly developed Stanford-Binet scale for determining the human Intelligence Quotient (IQ) gave no evidence of any tendency toward higher IQs in males than in females. Hollingworth started with that discovery. But there were no studies yet published that disproved another of Professor Thorndike's postulates: males were more likely to be "eminent" and also more likely to be "idiots" because there was a greater "variability" inherent in the male segment of the population. This well-entrenched theory held that there was a greater tendency among males to move to either extreme on the scale of intelligence; conversely, the theory assigned a status of general mediocrity to women.

Thorndike and other proponents of the theory of greater male variability rested their case on two facts: there were more men than women in institutions for the feebleminded, and there were also more men than women in positions of eminence. Lacking any prior studies to cite in discrediting this pernicious theory, Leta Hollingworth set out to see what some original research might uncover.

Though she could not dispute the fact that more males than females were wards of institutions for the feebleminded, she did what no one else had bothered to do—she investigated the reasons for the overabundance of male inmates. In an article in the *American Journal of Sociology* in 1914, she set forth her findings. More males were institutionalized, Hollingworth said, because feebleminded, or mentally retarded, men were more likely to be a nuisance rather than a help if kept within the home, and they generally could not support themselves outside the home. Therefore, feeblemindedness in males was usually recognized at a relatively young age and was generally seen as an insurmountable handicap that warranted institutionalization.

Conversely, feeblemindedness in women could be more easily tolerated in the home, and retarded females were often kept at home to do the simple household chores that their 6- or 7-year-old minds could easily learn and their adult bodies could easily perform. Such women could even support themselves outside the home by cooking, scrubbing, washing, ironing, and tending little children. Some married and bore children of their own, their weak minds proving no obstacle to men who sought only a warm and loving body, an adequate domestic laborer, and the promise of offspring. Only in their later years, when they grew too old for domestic duties or were widowed and left penniless, were they likely to be admitted to institutions. Thus there were not more feebleminded men than women. There were simply more institutionalized feebleminded males than females, hardly a proof of greater variability of males.

But this argument only disproved half of Thorndike's theory. The professor also proposed that the mediocrity of women was proved by the "likeness" or "sameness" of housewives and mothers and by a general "lack of eminence" in women. In countering this charge, Hollingworth asserted that the "likeness" of housewives and mothers would be matched by a "likeness" among men, had they all been preordained to be farmers and fathers. Furthermore, she maintained that any lack of eminence in women could be laid to the fact that even the brightest and best were relegated to a single career— that of housewife and mother. Thus, lack of eminence did not prove that women were innately ill-suited to eminence; it merely proved that

> housekeeping and the rearing of children, though much commended to women as proper fields for the exploitation of their talents, are, unfortunately for their fame, not fields in which eminence can be attained. No one knows, for instance, who at present is the best housekeeper in America, nor who has borne and reared the finest family of children.

Hollingworth had in effect destroyed the theory of greater male variability. But she went one step farther. With Helen Montague, M. D., she examined 2,000 newborns, performing tests that showed that there was no greater physical variability among boys at birth than among girls. Their experiments also suggested, though they did not prove, that neither was there a greater mental variability. Hollingworth and Montague maintained that since measurements of such traits as mental competence and leadership ability had to be made later in life, measurements of such traits could not be used as proof of inherent sex differences, since " 'a sex difference' . . . can be called inherent only if present when training and environment are similar," and training and environment of males and females were not likely to be similar, given society's preconceived notions of sex differences.

In 1914, 4 short years after Hollingworth broke out of her New

York apartment determined to resume a meaningful life for herself, she published her doctoral dissertation, a widely acclaimed study that toppled another theoretical base of male superiority. *Functional Periodicity* struck the first effective blow at the centuries-old notion that a woman of childbearing age is unfit for mental or physical work during the days of her menstrual period. Using objective research findings, Hollingworth disproved a theory that had been originally founded and heretofore defended solely upon the basis of subjective evidence. In daring to test and disprove this widely accepted theory, she made use of research methods that characterized all of her work as psychologist, sociologist, and educator.

Functional Periodicity was a landmark work, for all previous writings on the subject had been by men, and Hollingworth realized that "since the phenomenon of periodicity was foreign to them, they not unnaturally seized upon it as a probable source of the alleged 'mystery' and 'caprice' of womankind. The dogma once formulated has been quoted on authority from author to author until the present day." To her it seemed highly ironic that men who would never have presumed "to write authoritatively on any other subject regarding which they possessed no reliable or expert knowledge, have not hesitated to make the most positive statements regarding the mental and motor abilities of women as related to functional periodicity."

Before publishing her own theory, Hollingworth had engaged in extensive research. By testing the mental and motor abilities of women both during and outside their menstrual periods and comparing tests results with those of men, Hollingworth showed that women were no more or less skilled or efficient workers at various times of the month than were men. On the basis of her research, she concluded that any limitations individual women might display during their menstrual periods were probably due to sociological, not biological, reasons.

She invited others to follow her lead in disproving other theories of this ilk, noting that "it seems appropriate and desirable that women should investigate these matters experimentally, now that the opportunity for training and research is open." She hoped such investigation would, in time, lead to a psychology of women based "on precise, not on anecdotal evidence, on accurate data rather than on remnants of magic."

Her own studies on the psychology of women, among the first undertaken by a woman trained in science, earned her a position of authority among feminists. As might be expected, she joined in the fight for women's suffrage, though she later said she felt suffrage was important "not as a cause of change but as a sign of change in status."

In a 1927 article called "New Woman in the Making," she traced the development of woman's status through the centuries, then noted that "Each woman, even now, who sets out upon a way of life different from that of the dependent housewife, is still an explorer. . . ." According to Hollingworth, woman's major question of the future would be learning how

> to reproduce the species and at the same time to win satisfaction of the human appetites for food, security, self-assertion, mastery, adventure, [and] play. Man satisfies these cravings by competitive attack, both physical and mental, upon the environment. As compared with man, woman has always been in a cage with these satisfactions outside. The cage has been her cumbersome reproductive system.

In a 1916 article in the *American Journal of Sociology* she cited the various devices society has developed for keeping woman in her cage by compelling her to bear and rear children in order to perpetuate the race, noting that without such devices most women would have given up motherhood as far too burdensome and bothersome a state. Citing the power and beauty of the "maternal instinct," society had made it normal and commendable to become a mother, and law, religion, education, and art had all conspired to present the madonna image as the ideal. Yet, according to Hollingworth, "maternal instinct," if indeed there was any such instinct, would likely vary so greatly in intensity from woman to woman as to be almost nonexistent in some. Hollingworth predicted that "as soon as women become fully conscious of the fact that they have been and are controlled by these devices, the . . . [devices] will become useless," and only then will there be available a true indication of the nature and strength of "maternal instinct."

Though confident that enough women would still desire motherhood to give the world enough babies, she warned that once women are in control of their reproductive systems and aware of their options, society must be prepared to offer "adequate compensation, either in money or fame," if a surplus of babies is desired. Such a suggestion must certainly have seemed radical in 1916, yet to Leta Hollingworth it was a perfectly rational solution to an issue that had always been handled emotionally, and she maintained that "If these matters could be clearly raised to consciousness, so that this aspect of human life could be managed rationally . . . the social gain would be enormous—assuming always that the increased happiness and usefulness of women would, in general, be considered a social gain."

Leta Stetter Hollingworth's major contributions toward that much-needed social gain were made from 1911 to 1914 while she pursued graduate work in educational psychology and earned a teacher's certificate from Columbia Teachers College. By the time she was ready to receive her PhD, she had moved on to pioneering work in still another field.

Upon receipt of her M.A. degree, she was offered a one-year position as a substitute for the regular administrator of several newly designed mental tests at a hospital for the mentally retarded. Her ability to work well with staff and patients, her keen sense of scientific precision and caution, and her rare gift of expressing and interpreting test results made her work so highly valued that she was asked to continue on the staff even after the regular administrator returned.

Her position in the mental hospital was that of a clinical psychologist, and she was openly critical of many of her fellow practitioners. She had high standards in testing procedures, and she decried the superficiality of the methods many clinical psychologists were using. Group tests, she maintained, "are useful only when limited to what they can properly do, which is to give an approximate picture of the ability of a group." The psychologist who wished to learn the IQ of a particular child must be willing to test that child in person and to study the child under the pressure of that testing.

Arguing that far too many psychologists were more interested in studying tests than in studying children, she cautioned that " 'the whole child' cannot be studied in absentia, nor, for that matter, can any part of him be so studied." For her, a psychological study was always the study of an individual, a concept that was hailed as a new approach in the 1940s but that had been Leta Hollingworth's approach from her earliest days of practice. Partly because of her desire to foster that approach, she became a founding member of the American Association of Clinical Psychology and worked to help that group upgrade the standards of the profession.

In May of 1916, at age 30, Hollingworth received her PhD in clinical psychology from Columbia; she was offered the position of chief of the psychological laboratory being opened that summer at Bellevue Hospital. Still drawn to teaching, she turned down the Bellevue offer to accept an instructorship in educational psychology at Columbia Teachers College, a position that carried with it the responsibility for continuing the work underway there with exceptional children. At that time, the term "exceptional" was most often applied to those who fell below the norm in IQ. Dr. Hollingworth had been working with these children as a graduate student, and by 1916 she had already published a half-dozen scientific papers concerning the relationship between mental ability, school performance, and social adjustment.

As her work with subnormal children was enlarged upon over the next few years, her experience in administering IQ tests proved to be an invaluable aid in her research. One of the first persons in the country to use the Binet test as a means of determining the needs and characteristics of subnormal children, she was convinced that early diagnosis of feeblemindedness and adequate follow-up work with children so diagnosed were essential if problems in later life were to be avoided.

In 1920, Dr. Hollingworth published *The Psychology of Subnormal Children*, a work reprinted yearly for the next decade and long considered the standard text on the topic. Stressing her belief that intelligence was "the ability to adapt behavior to the successful attainment of desired ends," the book presented the clinical data on subnormal children in such a way as to make it meaningful to classroom teachers. Explaining the psychology of the feebleminded in terms of the individual child, she stressed the fact that the feebleminded differ from ordinary children not in kind, but in degree. The feebleminded child simply fails to progress far enough along the ordinary path of mental development. Thus no unique materials or methods are required in the task of training these youngsters, since they can learn the same things other children learn—up to a point. While Dr. Hollingworth's theories on the progression of mental development were considered avant-garde for her own time, today they form the basis for the "readiness tests" and developmental scales that are widely administered to determine mental and physical maturity levels of young children.

By the '20s, Dr. Hollingworth had become the leading authority in the psychology and education of subnormal children. She established special classes for subnormal children in several communities and served as adviser to those in charge of such classes in New York City and in other cities across the country and abroad.

Her work with subnormal children made her increasingly aware of another area in which changes in educational curricula were needed—the area of educating those with special talents and those with learning disabilities in specific subject areas. In 1922 she published *Special Talents and Defects: Their Significance for Education.* That same year she joined Teachers College colleagues in an experiment in homogeneous grouping, an experiment destined to change the course of her career.

Public School 165 was chosen for a 3-year study in which 2 groups of gifted children were placed in special classes, a move that provided the psychologists and educators who worked with those classes a unique opportunity to study the phenomenon of bright children and to provide the children being studied with educational experiences designed to meet their special needs. These youngsters, 7 to 9 years old, were taught regular classroom subjects, but were given "enrichment classes" as well.

Over a 3-year period, Dr. Hollingworth and her colleagues studied the origins, backgrounds, and family characteristics of the 50 children enrolled in the P.S. 165 program. They examined their psychological characteristics, their physical, social, educational, and temperamental traits, and the course of their development. Then, for nearly 20 years thereafter, they studied their subsequent growth and charted their vocational and economic progress.

The general public was not responsive to Hollingworth's work in this area, for as an egalitarian nation, Americans tended to deny individual differences, particularly extreme ones. But the enrichment classes seemed entirely justifiable to Dr. Hollingworth, since she felt that those who were above normal in ability deserved the same opportunity to reach their highest potential as did those who were subnormal. To those who believed such a system was undemocratic, Hollingworth replied that "true idealism demands impersonal truth as a basis for action," adding that she found it "inconceivable that the blind wish to believe that all men are created equal will prevail over demonstrated truth."

Out of this experiment, Dr. Hollingworth published 32 papers in educational journals and produced *Gifted Children* (1926), a work destined to become the standard text in this latest specialty area of educational psychology. In these works she explained that "by a gifted child we mean one who is far more educable than the generality of children are" and stressed that the giftedness might be in the arts, in mechanical aptitude, or "in surpassing power to achieve literary and abstract knowledge." Dr. Hollingworth's studies showed that excellence in one area is usually predictive of excellence in nearly all other areas and that current educational practice did not provide a sufficiently challenging program for most gifted children. Stressing the fact that "intellectually gifted children are among the most valuable assets of a civilized nation," she urged support of programs that would avoid wasting this valuable resource.

In 1934, having studied the children of P.S. 165 for a dozen years and having already laid the groundwork for continued observation of them and of their offspring for several decades to come, Dr. Hollingworth gave over her energies to the design and administration of P.S. 500, the Speyer School, a school that would be devoted exclusively to the education of exceptional children.

Dr. Hollingworth agreed to undertake this responsibility on the condition that the children enrolled in this school should come from varied backgrounds. She was well aware that the children in her special classes at P.S. 165 had been members of a single census group and had not in any way represented a cross section of the city's children. Her stipulations were met, and the classes of P.S. 500 mirrored the general ethnic, socioeconomic, and racial makeup of New York's public schools. The school opened on February 3, 1936, with 225 students; 175 children with IQs of 75 to 90 were grouped together in common classes, as were 50 children with IQs of 130 or above.

Dr. Hollingworth had long advocated "fitting the school to the child," and the Speyer School gave her a unique opportunity to test her theories. In a child's life span, she said, the years from ages 7 to 13 were the "Golden Age of the Intellect" because this was the age of questioning, and her programs at the Speyer School were designed to foster the questionings. Curious children were led to pursue the answers to their own questions. She believed that children should be encouraged in initiative and originality, and her enrichment program sought to impart those traits.

Students in her gifted classes spent half their time on typical school subjects, with some extra work in French and nutrition, then devoted the other half to enrichment projects based on the theme "The Evolution of Common Things." The children themselves chose the "common things" whose evolution should be studied—from food and clothing to communications and travel—and they used the resources of nearby libraries and universities to prepare reports and special projects on these topics. Hollingworth watched these children flourish under the new system, joying in her observations, for, as her husband said, "A bright mind at work was to her a spectacle of compelling beauty."

Hollingworth was also discovering that the needs of the bright child could be great, especially in the case of the highly gifted child.

By her judgment the "potential geniuses" of IQ 180 and above were
not entirely lucky in their brilliance. She found that such children
have fewer playmates with whom they can identify and a cor-
respondingly greater tendency to be lonely, cynical individuals. At
the time of her death she was beginning the final evaluation of 12
children with IQs over 180 whom she herself had managed to locate
and study, and under her husband's guidance *Children Above 180
IQ* was brought out in 1942, 3 years after her death.

Dr. Hollingworth believed that gifted and highly gifted girls had
particularly difficult adjustment problems, for they realized early
on they were "of the wrong sex" and from "a thousand tiny ways
they learn that they are not expected to entertain the same ambitions as their brothers." Adjustment was doubly hard for gifted children of the poor, whether male or female, since those children could
sense what they might attain, yet lacked the resources to reach their
full potential.

For such children, Leta Hollingworth advocated the establishment of loans and scholarships, but her pleas were largely ignored;
she could not overcome the prevailing misconception that the gifted
"can fend for themselves." Unable to disabuse either government
sources or private philanthropies of that well-ingrained prejudice,
she did not live to see the National Merit Scholars program open the
doors of the nation's universities to highly gifted adolescents who
could not otherwise have continued their education.

Dr. Hollingworth's interest in adolescents was not restricted to
"exceptional" teens. She was keenly and personally aware of the
adjustment problems common to this age group, having had a troubled, unhappy adolescence herself. She devoted several years to a
systematic study of the psychology of the adolescent and published
more than a dozen professional papers on the subject.

In 1928 she brought out *Psychology of the Adolescent*, a work
that one colleague called "the most penetrating analysis ever offered
of the characteristics, problems, and educational needs of all types
of teen-aged individuals, normal and unstable, bright and dull, tal-
ented and defective. . . ." While others had dismissed the emotional

upheavals of the adolescent as a natural consequence of physiological and chemical forces associated with sexual maturation, Dr. Hollingworth viewed these upheavals as the outward manifestations of the inner turmoil generated by a teen's efforts to solve tangible problems of adjustment.

She urged parents, educators, and teens themselves to view adolescence as a period of transition, a period of moving from obedience and dependence to self-determination and self-support. She maintained that these transitions pose more problems for adolescents in a highly developed society than for teens in more primitive cultures because in advanced cultures societal expectations made it "impossible to mate, to earn a living, and to exercise self-determination at the biologically appropriate time." Under such circumstances, Hollingworth felt that adolescent frustrations were inevitable. She urged the establishment of guidance clinics designed "to assist youth in finding the way to adulthood."

She saw the road to maturity as being particularly difficult for girls, since society did not foster independence in women, preferring to keep females at least semi-dependent. Although girls had the same diverse interests and abilities as boys, they were usually not permitted to choose both marital love and a profession. She encouraged permitting girls "to work out the relation between work and love by intelligent experimentation."

In the year *Psychology of the Adolescent* was published, Dr. Hollingworth was promoted to full professor and was granted a spring sabbatical. During her months on leave, she traveled to various European countries and studied their educational systems, concerning herself particularly with the ways in which those systems dealt with subnormal and with gifted children. She saw that while European children were educated to their full potential, that potential was seen as differing from individual to individual, and the length and breadth of educational experiences differed accordingly.

In Dr. Hollingworth's view, such a system was more democratic and ultimately more kind than the American system, which attempted to force all students, whatever their ability level, into the same educational mold and devised laws to detain even the least able in school until they reached a specified age or achieved a specified degree. She urged fellow educators to change the American system, to take steps to stop the loss and frustration that resulted when children of vastly unequal abilities were all educated in precisely the same manner.

In this stance she was again reminding those who worked with children to consider "the whole child" and to study the behavior and abilities of each child rather than relying on data concerning the behavior and abilities of an "average" human being of that age. As one colleague observed, "This intense interest in and devotion to the living individual, combined with the clear-eyed vision of the scientist, accounts for the unique scientific validity and practical value of her contribution [to the field of child psychology]." Partly because of her constant prodding, the fledgling science of psychology began to move in new directions, away from the study of abstract facts and principles and toward studies based on personal interaction between the psychologist and the individual.

Leta Hollingworth's interest in looking at the individual had evolved early in life. As a 20-year-old she had observed that everyone must give his life to something—and had seen as dismal the prospect of giving one's life to "things." Even then, she had seen clearly what her own choice must be, writing, "As for me, I think I could care above all things to have my life absorbed by human beings—just to give as much as I have to people . . . since give it somewhere we all must."

An accomplished poet, she left dreams of a career in writing behind her and devoted her energies to working with individual lives. From the tiny, triangular-shaped cubbyhole that served as her office, she conducted research, carried on consultations, advised students, supervised dissertations, and wrote the papers that made her findings and her insights available to others.

In 1937 the University of Nebraska recognized her and her husband for a lifetime of unselfish giving, awarding both Hollingworths honorary LLD degrees for their contributions to the fields of education and psychology. On that journey back home, Leta Hollingworth may well have been aware that she would not again visit the prairie lands of her childhood, for she took time to choose her burial spot in Lincoln's Wyuka Cemetery, declaring the East "too alien for purposes of eternal sleep."

Ten years earlier doctors had discovered a tumor, but when told it was probably not malignant, Hollingworth had chosen to avoid potentially debilitating surgery. For the decade that followed, she lived fully, apparently giving no further thought to her health. But in late 1939, overly exhausted, she asked for and was granted a leave of absence. Rest did not restore her strength, she grew rapidly worse, and exploratory surgery revealed inoperable abdominal cancer. Within three weeks she was dead—at age 53.

Though she herself had accepted with graciousness the idea of an early death, to her husband, colleagues, and students, her sudden loss was a great and tragic shock. Considered to be one of America's most distinguished psychologists, she had already written a half-dozen authoritative texts and nearly 100 technical and popular articles, all of which made significant contributions to her profession. Yet, as a dynamic woman of middle age, she seemed to have some of her greatest work still before her.

Believing that a memorial advancing the work to which she had devoted a lifetime would be the most proper form of tribute, her colleagues honored her with a memorial edition of *Teachers College Record*, an edition that set forth her contributions in several important areas and pointed those who followed toward work yet to be done in each of those areas.

The breadth of her influence and the significance of her accomplishments in so many areas seem to bear out her own assessment concerning the gifted—for such people, success in one area is usually predictive of success in most others. Though aware that her status as a female made her work somewhat more difficult, Leta Hollingworth never used this fact as an excuse for lack of accomplishment. Yet she was quite modest about her achievements. Often asked the reasons behind her success, she addressed that question in a brief autobiographical sketch:

I do not know. I was intellectually curious, I worked hard, was honest except for those minor benign chicaneries which are occasionally necessary when authority is stupid, disliked waste, and was never afraid to undertake an experiment or to change my mind. My family motto, translated from the Latin, reads, I love to test. Perhaps that is the explanation.

Indeed, Leta Stetter Hollingworth's entire life might well be considered a test, an ongoing experiment, for as she herself noted, "The New Woman of today is consciously experimenting with her own life to find the Good Life—surely this requires a courage and a genius deserving something better than blame or jeers, deserving at least open-minded toleration and assistance."

In the eyes of those whose lives were changed, whose opportunities were broadened due to the experimental life she herself lived, Leta Stetter Hollingworth's bold experiment in living deserved not only tolerance and assistance but applause and gratitude.

~ *Mary McDowell* ~
The Settlement Lady

*T*he brisk winds of late September whipped at the skirts of the sturdy lady who clambered down from the wagon and stepped deftly over a muddy rut onto the slatted boards that ran the short length of Gross Avenue. She eyed the colorless clapboard building before her, then turned to survey her surroundings with some trepidation. Just up the street, the way she'd come, was the intersection of Ashland and 47th, the heart of Packingtown, the end of the streetcar line, the end of the pavement, the end of the dreams of many immigrant families. Down the hard-packed street, Gross Avenue ended in the Union Stockyards, a square mile of pens, slaughterhouses, and packing plants, a square mile that dominated the life of Packingtown.

Mary McDowell turned back toward the tenement. Somewhere in the rear of this unpromising building was the apartment, four small *rooms that were to become the University of Chicago Settlement House.*

She looked back for just a moment at the wagon half-filled with boxes—books and bedding mostly—then quickly decided to survey the premises empty-handed, to see her future, dream her dream unencumbered by the necessities of the moment. Forward through the unlatched door and up the littered stairway. Second floor rear. She fumbled with the key she'd been given, a useless key, anyway, she thought, if she were to establish an open-door policy from the beginning.

Her fumblings roused some attention. First one, then another door opened down the hallway and hesitant figures emerged. Smiling uneasily at the timid gathering in the hallway, she leaned stalwartly against the reluctant door and broke through. Her Scottish instinct for order recoiled at the sight before her. Well, she'd known it would take some adjustment. One just doesn't move from Evanston to Packingtown without noticing some change in environment, some difference in decor. She'd learn to live with this if she was to grow to be one of them. And no one ever so desired to be one with her community as Mary McDowell desired to be accepted by her neighbors "back of the yards."

So this is where she'd begin, here in these rooms strewn now with the remnants of the last occupants—a broken crib, empty bottles, and rusty cans. McDowell walked to the window and looked out the dirty panes at the scene that spread below and before her. In 1894 Packingtown was the blight of Chicago, but it was the teeming home of thousands of immigrants who eked out a living in the yards and packing plants.

But not all of them were able to eke out a living, as these littered rooms silently testified. Some—hopeless, defeated—moved out, most likely into even more crowded quarters with another family; few, very few, moved several blocks south onto the flat prairie that opened where Chicago ended. There a few small homes, investments of the more properous residents of Packingtown, were beginning to appear.

McDowell turned back. She'd become familiar soon enough with the world out there. Time now to get settled, to make herself at home, to get on with the work of being a neighbor and friend to the men, women, and children of the world "back of the yards."

Mary McDowell had grown up in Fulton, Ohio, just east of Cincinnati, on the broad grassy banks of the Ohio River, and in light of the world in which children back of the yards spent their formative years, her childhood environment seemed idyllic. Yet buried within those pastoral scenes were all the influences that had brought her inexorably to Packingtown.

Born November 30, 1854, Mary Eliza McDowell was the eldest of 6 children of Malcolm McDowell and Jane Gordon McDowell. Most of her childhood was spent in the large, almost baronial house built by her grandfather Gordon, a shipbuilder, and she was raised in an awareness of the staunch American background of her ancestors, both the McDowells and the Gordons. Family stories always exemplified the wholesomeness of industry, the virtue of public service, and the importance of democracy, ideals that were to mark the style of the mature Mary McDowell.

Not as interested in his father-in-law's shipyards as in the new industry that was growing up around steel, Malcolm McDowell had briefly moved the family to Providence, Rhode Island, where he became the superintendent of an iron foundry. But at the outbreak of the Civil War he was called to Washington to serve on the staff of his older brother, General Irwin McDowell, and his wife and little ones returned to the family home in Fulton to wait out the war.

There the most active and formative years of Mary's girlhood were spent on the rolling lawns and dusty lanes that carried the citizens of Fulton from their homes to the boatyards, lumberyards, and tanneries that had grown up around the Gordon shipyards. In the middle years of the war her father was sent home from Washington to serve as military governor of Cincinnati.

He imparted to his daughter his devotion to the Union cause and his admiration for its leader, Abraham Lincoln. But Fulton, Ohio, was strongly Confederate in sympathies, and Mary's was sometimes a lonely position. Not that she needed allies to confirm her beliefs. She mounted her own personal boycott against her neighborhood grocer after she overheard him question Lincoln's integrity. And her sense of the righteousness of the president's principles was so outraged by an editorial criticizing him that she felt his honor vindicated only after she had waylaid and pummeled the newsboy for delivering such offensive material.

Her staunchly democratic ideals pervaded all, and she left the Episcopalian church where she had worshipped with her mother in rather aristocratic company to join the small Methodist chapel preferred by her father, where she felt quite at home surrounded by the simple, sturdy, life-filling faith of the working families of the Cincinnati waterfront.

Vivacious, imaginative, a frontier child by environment and by inclination, young Mary led a wholesome, out-of-doors existence, later recalling,

> As a child it always seemed to me a great waste of time to stop to eat or sleep. . . . We played under the shade of the great beech trees and at the side of the little stream that ran down the hill, or in rainy weather on the big porches—the whole neighborhood of children and myself. We had continuous plays that went on for days at a time.

She tolerated schoolwork, but barely, attending a one-room schoolhouse where her classmates were her playmates, children of the factory workers who lived as neighbors and who worked in paternalistic relationship with her grandfather and father. Her childhood also provided shared experiences with another group whose cause McDowell was later to foster—the blacks. She had strong attachments to the household servants whose work she shared, and shared willingly, since working alongside them made her a private audience to their homey and whimsical stories, stories that fed her imagination.

The postwar years found the McDowell family still growing and Malcolm McDowell yearning to leave the shipyards and be once again in the middle of the steel industry. The virility of Chicago attracted him, and by the beginning of the new decade he had settled his family in the northwest corner of that city. Many of the workers from Fulton followed him to Chicago, attracted by the promise of work in his new steel mill. A man of invention and achievement, Malcolm McDowell was almost a personification of the second industrial revolution that was reshaping American society. He gradually became a recognized expert in the steel industry; by the 1870s he was one of Chicago's most esteemed citizens, and he moved his family to Evanston, a fashionable suburb northeast of the city.

For all his status and activities, McDowell never lost the bond of friendship with his daughter, and Mary herself remained primarily a family-centered person. As she later wrote, "My education was obtained in the public and private schools of Ohio and Chicago, but mostly in being the oldest daughter of a large family. . . ." Such an education teaches an overriding concern for others and demands energetic and efficient action.

That these traits were already well formed in the young girl was evident in the aftermath of the great Chicago fire of 1871. For the two days that the fire raged, 17-year-old Mary drove the family's wagon back and forth between the burning city and the barren prairies bordering the McDowell home, carrying refugees and supplies.

In the wake of the tragedy, a patchwork town of rude shanties and tents grew up on the prairie, and in the days that followed, Mary worked among the displaced families of that impromptu settlement. In the absence of a central disbursing agency, efforts to distribute the food, clothing, and money that began to pour into Chicago from all parts of the country were at first haphazard. Rutherford B. Hayes, the governor of Ohio and a close friend of the McDowell family, directed his state's contributions to the McDowell home to be dispensed. Mary took over, and for the next few weeks her organizational talents and her unceasing efforts drew the attention and the admiration of municipal officials. When an official distribution agency, the Relief Aid Society, was at last established, Mary became a member and continued to work for the resurgence of the city and its people.

Though her family's needs kept her close to home for the next 20 years, she was active in her own sphere during that time. When Rutherford Hayes was elected president of the United States in 1876, 22-year-old Mary spent a month in Washington helping the new first family move into the White House.

With her father she continued her church work, conducting classes at the Methodist church in Evanston. Through her church group she met Frances Willard, who was then founding the Women's Christian Temperance Union. Working closely with her, McDowell was instrumental in the establishment of an auxiliary organization, the Young Women's Christian Temperance Union.

Around this same time McDowell became interested in a new concept in education—the kindergarten movement. She enrolled in Elizabeth Harrison's school, later to be called the National Kindergarten College, completed the course, and moved briefly to New York City as a private tutor for a family.

When her mother's failing health drew her home, her background and her instincts soon led her to join in a new experiment underway in Chicago. In 1889 Jane Addams and Ellen Star had founded a "settlement house" in the old mansion of General Hull, located in an industrial section of Chicago. Dedicated to improving the living conditions of the poor, Hull House was an expression of a new spirit, a spirit filled with "high hopes and ardent wishes for social betterment." McDowell was drawn to the center shortly after its founding, and in 1890 she became a Hull House resident, establishing a kindergarten there. Her work with the little ones led her into contact with mothers, and before long she had organized the Hull House Woman's Club.

In 1893 her mother's worsened condition forced her to leave Hull House and return to the family home in Evanston. More and more frequently, conversations with her father and his friends centered around the growing unrest of the working people and the new phenomenon of unionism. These abstractions became harsh realities in 1894 when the Chicago area was rocked by the historic Pullman Strike, in which employees of the Pullman Palace Car Company struck to protest reduced wages that were not accompanied by re-

duced rents in company-owned housing. By refusing to handle Pullman cars, trainmen all over the country showed their sympathy with
the local strikers and focused the attention of the American public
on the plight of the workers.

Though Mary McDowell probed intensely for an understanding
of the issues embedded in the strike, she found no one in her circle
who could clarify, who could separate emotion and bias from fact,
and she later wrote that living as close as they were to "that great
seething restless Chicago where the workers, the mass of the population, were struggling," the people of Evanston still "saw no reason
why wage-earners who had work should be disturbing the peace of
our cultured community with its Browning societies and many
churches." In contrast, McDowell herself saw the Pullman strike as
only one aspect of "a great world of unrest which must be understood."

Preoccupied with the problems and hardships of Chicago's poor,
she began to question openly the structure of American society and
the changing role of American industry. Though the Pullman strike
was broken, McDowell's fervor to do something about the human
cost of industrial life was aroused. "In Evanston," she said, referring
to the interests of the community, "they knew all about temperance,
but very little about labor."

The ignorance of the citizens of Evanston was matched by the
general ignorance of all Americans. No investigations of any significance had ever been made into working conditions, hours, or wages.
Only a handful of universities in the country offered any courses in
the affairs of human welfare or the affairs of labor and industry, and
relatively few people had even heard the terms "social service" and
"sociology."

These terms were increasingly important to students and faculty
at the University of Chicago. Founded on the southern edge of the
city in 1891, the fledgling university had, by 1893, established a
department of sociology, the first such department in the country.
Faculty and students of the new department, interested in the
causes of contemporary unrest, decided to establish a kind of laboratory of social service in the city.

After surveying all its parts, they determined that the district just back of the Union Stockyards, a district that had been the scene of rioting and bloodshed during the Pullman strike just months before, was the area of the city most in need of a social center. Having determined the site, the group asked Jane Addams of Hull House to recommend a director. She endorsed Mary McDowell, citing her ready sympathy for the poor, her quick understanding, and her untiring labor. McDowell, then 40 years old, accepted the position quickly and enthusiastically. And in September of 1894, she moved to Gross Avenue to establish a settlement house in a walk-up flat back of the yards. Packingtown was to be her home for the next 42 years.

In the fall of 1894 Packingtown was a crude, ugly neighborhood. It was bordered on the north by the backwaters of the Chicago River, a brackish channel called "Bubbly Creek," and on the west by a vast open pit that served as the Chicago city dump. To the south lay flat, bedraggled prairie, and to the east stretched the "yards," a vast area of stockyards, packing plants, and railroad tracks that dominated the life of Packingtown. Only the two main streets of Packingtown—Ashland Avenue, appropriately known as Whisky Row, and 47th Street—were paved; the others were either dusty and littered or muddy and littered, depending on the season.

Houses, built close to the boardwalk, were crowded and colorless, stained to one drab tone by smoke and dirt. The grimness of Packingtown was unrelieved by any trees, grass, or shrubbery, and its stench pervaded all, a stench that was a blending of the odors of the rotting garbage dump, the brackish waters of Bubbly Creek, and the decaying refuse of the slaughterhouses and stockyards.

Packingtown's population represented almost every immigrant group. Many years later, in recalling the flavor of her neighborhood, McDowell observed that the population of the twenty-ninth ward doubled every 10 years and changed nationality every 15. Now in 1894 the Irish and the Germans predominated, but there were growing numbers of Poles and Bohemians, Lithuanians and Russians. Later the Scottish, Welsh, and English began to arrive. The immigrants arrived in waves and were caught in a mire of overcrowded, unsanitary housing, competitive employment, starvation wages, and unhealthy working conditions. Their bodies became crippled by the effects of tuberculosis and rheumatism, and their spirits demoralized by the crude conditions of their lives.

It was amid such surroundings and among such people that Mary McDowell came to live. Her work was to be financially supported by the University of Chicago, but she was free to decide for herself the form and the spirit that work should take. Its form and spirit were quickly evident. McDowell went as a friend and as a neighbor with a "keen sense of the commonness of all." From her earliest report she sensed her direction: "The task of the Settlement is to be the wise, understanding, and generous neighbor of a large population of foreign origin who help do the work and share the destinies of Chicago and the United States."

At first she was an intriguing, mysterious figure to her neighbors, but she did not long remain a stranger. She was in every sense a large woman; she glowed with warmth and she sparkled with humor. She quickly won their confidence, and they were soon referring to her as "the Settlement Lady." In an editorial that noted the existence of the new settlement house, a Chicago newspaperman wrote of McDowell: "Her life is becoming incorporated in the life of the community in which she lives; she is developing a neighborhood consciousness; she does not stay, but she lives, in the stockyards region and is learning to say 'we' unconsciously."

Her first activities were varied. She opened a day nursery and a kindergarten. The reservations of the shy, suspicious parents were quickly overcome by the enthusiasm of the children and the warmth and energy of "the Settlement Lady." As she had done at Hull House, McDowell soon drew the mothers into the Woman's Club, her first organization for adults. That group drew up and circulated a petition calling for the establishment of a public bathhouse for the Packingtown area. When the City Fathers acceded to the demands and built a bathhouse, the residents had their first taste of political power.

Flushed with the success of this project, the settlement organized the Civic Improvement Association. Although the twenty-ninth ward was the site of the municipal garbage dump, its residents were being denied city garbage service, and their accumulated refuse threatened to bury Packingtown. After much agitation, the city fathers finally, "to quiet them women," sent out inspectors. The inspectors were closely followed by city cleaning crews, which swept through Packingtown's alleys, removing debris and whitewashing fences.

The Civic Improvement Association, now thoroughly convinced of what the city could be made to do, became a vital organization, more and more insistent on municipal funds and services to cope with the infinite problems of congested urban life. With every victory, McDowell was forging the settlement into a permanent factor of life back of the yards. Her neighborly spirit was the germ and the soul of a new community consciousness.

The settlement grew because it provided a pathway to a quality of life the Packingtown residents alone had not been able to achieve, even aspire to. Within months of her arrival in Packingtown, McDowell had to enlist university students as volunteer, part-time assistants to help her staff all the activities that had sprung up around the settlement house. These volunteers made possible wider programs and necessitated larger quarters. A year after it first opened, the settlement took occupancy of another floor of the Gross Avenue tenement. And a year after that, it relocated to a floor over a feed store on Ashland Avenue and spilled over into a nearby storeroom.

The living room over the feed store housed a lending library, which, with pressure from McDowell, soon became an official branch of the Chicago Public Library. It was also the scene of free Sunday concerts given by artists from all over the city. The settlement house hosted literary, dramatic, and artistic programs. The Settlement Lady cornered funds from agencies and friends to provide these and other services. The packers themselves, who did not fail to notice the work of their new neighbor, provided the salary of a resident nurse who visited the sick, taught parents new ways to provide for their infants, and gave classes in nutrition and hygiene.

The phenomenal growth continued. In 1897, barely 3 years after its founding, the settlement's future was all but assured when the

directors of the university board approved the purchase of two lots
on Gross Avenue, directly across the street from the tenement that
first housed McDowell. There, on one of the lots a gymnasium was
built, a multipurpose building that served as auditorium, theater,
classroom, meeting hall, church, and dance hall. Such a building
enlarged the scope of the settlement activities. Five years later, on
the second lot another, even larger, building was opened, giving the
settlement all the necessary facilities for a library and a savings
bank; for concerts, lectures, and exhibitions; and for club meetings,
union meetings, and classes. The new addition also provided living
quarters for permanent residents of the staff and for transient residents of Packingtown.

McDowell's imagination and inventiveness enabled her to convert
the most meager of resources to the most grandiose accomplishments. When pressured by the Chicago Police Department to do
something about the mischief of the children who loitered, idle and
bored, on the dusty streets of Packingtown, the alderman of the
twenty-ninth ward offered McDowell $25 to "do something." She
promptly converted that paltry sum into the beginnings of a magnifi-
cent system of city playgrounds.

The project started inauspiciously enough. With her $25 Mc-
Dowell bought and filled a sandbox and built one swing on an
empty corner lot across from the settlement house. That preliminary
playground showed such promise that McDowell went to Boston to
study a well-established system of city parks and came home to
incorporate new ideas in her corner lot. Jane Addams of Hull House,
facing the same problem of youth in the streets, joined with Mc-
Dowell to pressure the city to provide funds for the park.

The idea of community recreation was sold to the public and to
the city commission. Nineteen neighborhood squares were planned
and built. Davis Square, Packingtown's own park, was constructed
in 1904, and its dedication was marked by a "festival of play" in
which every nationality of the neighborhood was represented in a
jumble of folk dances, songs, and athletic contests.

McDowell's concept of playgrounds and parks also led to the
development of Buckingham Gardens, a project unique to Packing-

town. With the opening of Davis Square, some blocks away, the settlement converted its own corner playground into garden plots, an idea and activity that became so popular that Clarence Buckingham, owner of several vacant lots near the settlement, offered his property for additional gardens. For a penny a week, a child was given a small square of ground to plant and cultivate as he wished. In one of her periodic reports, McDowell noted that in Buckingham Gardens "the cultivation of children quite as much as the cultivation of plants took place."

From the earliest days education had been a primary thrust of the settlement. Soon after the establishment of a kindergarten, Mc-Dowell had turned to meeting the needs of her adult neighbors, whose great interest seemed to be in learning the language of their new country and in becoming citizens. The settlement began to organize classes in language, history, civics, and literature. Teachers qualified to work with non-English-speaking adults and with special materials adapted to their needs were pressed into service.

In these "schools of citizenship" students were divided into groups according to their previous educational experience and were instructed in their own languages in elementary principles of government. As they achieved a certain level of understanding they were taken by a settlement sponsor to the naturalization office to obtain their citizenship. Within a few years the settlement had formulated a very successful program—the model of which formed the basis of a system of adult education adopted by the Chicago public school system.

From the "schools of citizenship" the settlement branched out to experiment in other areas of education where needs were apparent. Early on, the settlement had secured a farm in Indiana where children could be sent for healthier months of summer than they could ever know in Packingtown. However, only limited numbers of children could benefit from that program, and hundreds of Packingtown's children still loitered on its streets in the idle summer months.

As part of her campaign against the problem of unoccupied youth, McDowell approached the Chicago school board. She was given a school building in which to run an experimental summer program. The idea was so successfully carried out that the next year the school board not only renewed the program but also supplied McDowell with funds for manual training equipment for her summer school. This idea had a permanent effect on the Chicago school system. Growing out of that early experiment in vocational education came public high schools devoted to the teaching of manual arts and domestic sciences.

Where childhood play and leisure activities for adults had been unknown, where school facilities and adult education had been inadequate, McDowell had raised new possibilities and was meeting unfulfilled needs. Jane Addams marvelled at her accomplishments and publicly cited her ability to "form new and hopeful combinations with the most unpromising of materials . . . and to suggest solutions for problems which the community had long accepted as insoluble."

But McDowell had realized early on that all of Packingtown's problems were directly related to the industry that shadowed the neighborhood. Ninety percent of the laborers who lived back of the yards worked in the great packing plants and stockyards, and every phase of their lives was touched by that industry. McDowell knew that she could not ignore the basic fact of the industrial character of Packingtown if she hoped to improve the quality of life of its residents.

Like all of American industry the packing industry had undergone phenomenal growth during the last years of the century. The Chicago stockyards district had become a world of its own, a world where the names of Armour and Swift represented forces of control over the lives of thousands of skilled and unskilled laborers. The working conditions within this world were all but intolerable, and in every activity McDowell undertook for the benefit of her community she saw their disastrous effects. "I was meeting with men who, 'for fear of losing a job,' went to and from work with a silent protest against conditions and a sense of injustice they were afraid to express," she wrote.

But the time had come for recognition of the human factor of production. The labor movement that the Pullman strike had first brought to McDowell's attention was silently growing back of the yards, and in 1901 the working men of Packingtown found a voice for their silent protest. That year Michael Donnelly, a butcher himself, came to the stockyards with his message of collective bargaining and social justice, and the framework of a union began to take shape. In the first years under Donnelly, collective bargaining brought about slightly higher wages—up to 18.5 cents per hour for unskilled labor and 40 cents per hour for skilled—and improved working conditions, advances that immeasurably increased the morale of Packingtown.

McDowell quickly saw the value of the work Donnelly was doing, espoused his cause, and spread his ideals of unionism among the women workers. Together she and Donnelly formed a union for the women—the Amalgamated Meat Cutter and Butcher Workmen of America, Local 183. Fifteen hundred strong, the women's union became a social as well as an industrial force in the community. For Mary McDowell, unionism was not an end in itself. It was, rather, a means to the one end toward which she had devoted her energies since 1894—the betterment of living conditions for Packingtown's people.

Her faith in the promise of the union movement was tested to its depth in the bitter strike of 1904. In mid-June, facing the industry's proposed cut in the wages of unskilled workers, Donnelly called his union out on strike. It began as an orderly walkout. From the beginning, McDowell endorsed the strike as the only means to protect hard-won advances in human dignity. There was no question of her support, for she believed that "Labor needs spokesmen . . . [and] I think I could do no better than to . . . do all in my power to make the public understand the human and social side of this industrial dispute."

In the early days, the strike was such a peaceful contention that the public took to calling it "Miss McDowell's pink tea strike." But hard lines were drawn as the summer moved on and no settlement was reached. Knowing that the Settlement Lady risked loss of considerable moral and financial support if she continued to endorse the strike, Packingtown residents laid bets as to whether "she'd stick or not."

McDowell stuck. Through a long, hot summer, when tension mounted and uncertainty gripped Packingtown, McDowell spoke out whenever she could find an audience, always advocating non-violence, yet always advocating the workers' position. "The public will have to learn that Michael Donnelly represents as important an interest as the packers," she said.

In the end, hunger decided the strike in favor of industry. By September, McDowell sensed the despair of the strike leaders and knew the workers could not hold out much longer. She joined Jane Addams and Cornelia deBey, a Chicago physician active in social causes, in requesting an interview with J. Ogden Armour, the representative of the packing interests. At that meeting the women proposed a face-saving scenario for the settlement of the strike; the packers agreed to meet with representatives of the unions. The unions were forced to accept industry's original terms, but the workers came back to their jobs "with their [union] buttons on."

"The strike failed but not dishonorably," said Mary McDowell. "The cause of the unskilled and the underpaid is not dead—it will keep forcing itself to the surface because it is a . . . question that deals with the raising of a standard of living."

Realizing that only strong unions could command better wages, hours, and working conditions, McDowell had embraced unionism. But she soon came to realize that the plight of women in the work force was a problem apart from ordinary labor problems, and she launched a new crusade. "We are not cheered when outsiders talk about equality of men and women in the economic field for we know that at present there is no such equality . . . ," she declared, "[for men do not] bear the children, care for the homemaking and work for wages all at the same time."

Shortly after the Great Strike, she and Jane Addams made a personal visit to the White House to press Theodore Roosevelt for a Congressional investigation into all aspects of the working woman's life. Having gained Roosevelt's promise of support, McDowell traveled nationally, enlisting the aid of unions, women's clubs, and politicians in lobbying for federal legislation guaranteeing the rights and protection of workers, particularly working women and children. Her efforts led to legislation appropriating funds for a massive 4-year study. Published in 1911, the findings of that study were considered for many years afterward the most authoritative picture of the conditions in American industry.

During the years that followed, individual states across the country considered various legislative bills intended to provide for the rights of women in industry, and the bills drew McDowell's interest and support. Under the auspices of the Women's Trade Union League she traveled to state capitals in Ohio, Maryland, Pennsylvania, Massachusetts, Michigan, and Alabama, in each case pressing hard for the passage of the legislation she knew to be essential to improving the lives of working families.

But improving the lives of working families back of the yards was in all these years her primary concern. And that concern carried her into many areas. Packingtown was a black mark on the health chart of the city of Chicago; its disease and death rates were the highest of the city. Its infant mortality rate was almost unbelievable—one in 3 children died before reaching the age of 3.

McDowell's early response to this problem had been to provide hygiene and nutrition education for parents, but she realized the inadequacy of these measures. The causes of disease and death were multiple, and she undertook an intensive survey of the health hazards of her neighborhood. The survey quickly led her to the most probable sources: the blighted environment that bordered Packingtown—Bubbly Creek on the north and the municipal garbage dump on the west.

She attacked these sources of human misery in the same way and in the same spirit with which she attacked all other problems besetting her neighborhood. She mustered all the investigative power and political forces at her disposal. In fighting for closure of the city dump, she organized committees, circulated petitions, and made reports to City Hall. She was no sanitation expert, but she became one, and a figure of considerable municipal influence as well. As she had earlier gone to Boston to study the best system of playgrounds, now she trekked to Europe to study the advanced systems of waste disposal in the larger cities of England, Scotland, Holland, and Germany.

Returning with facts, figures, and pictures, she mounted public opinion and badgered officials. She was at first thwarted by empty promises, but in the end a commission was appointed to study the various options for municipal waste disposal. Mary McDowell, by now "the Garbage Lady," was a member of the commission, which at the end of its study recommended that the city of Chicago build and operate reduction plants to dispose of municipal garbage. In such plants, refuse was dried or cooked to eliminate its liquid content, and the converted waste was then suitable for use as fill or as fertilizer. In 1913 a reduction plant was built in the open pit of Packingtown, and the dried waste from the plant was used to fill and grade the city's new lakefront area.

McDowell's campaign against the menace of Bubbly Creek required even more sustained effort than her fight to close the dump. Bubbly Creek was a stagnant pool covered by scum from the sewage of Packingtown homes and the refuse of the slaughterhouses. Putrescent gases forming below the surface of the scum bubbled their way through, giving the creek its name. Convinced that improving the health of Packingtown's people depended on solving the problem of Bubbly Creek, Mary McDowell went to each new city administration; she even took the problem to Congress. Her ceaseless efforts gained her one more title, "The Duchess of Bubbly Creek," but she was stymied on every front, year after year. Ironically, only when the great packing industry saw an advantage in reclaiming the land for its own purpose did the ugly and unsanitary pool disappear. Seeing a need for a rail spur across the creek, the packers had sewage collection pipes laid, and Bubbly Creek was filled in.

These hard-won advances in sanitation brought about a gradual improvement in Packingtown's overall health record. And they brought the Settlement Lady ever closer to her people. "There [has] come to me," she said, "a reverence for human beings and a humility in the presence of their struggles." In 1919, their struggles were manifested in violence, and Mary McDowell was caught up in the ugliness of race riots. From 1910, blacks had been immigrating to Chicago in ever-increasing numbers, and their arrival had brought new problems, revived and enlarged old ones, and complicated the already confused pattern of social, civic, and industrial existence in her neighborhood.

The black migration swelled the Negro area of Chicago and pushed southward to the borders of the twenty-ninth ward, where conflicts between the Polish and Irish of Packingtown and the blacks became almost constant. Then, in the hot summer of 1919, smoldering animosity erupted into violence that engulfed the city. Carrying a gospel of understanding and good will, McDowell appealed to her neighbors to restore peace to the city, decrying the loss of life, the destruction of property, the insanity of the hatred.

In the aftermath of the riots, she gained the respect and trust of all parties to the issue. Her work to bring about racial harmony was always focused on bringing the opposing groups together. Alain Locke, a philosopher and black leader, said of her:

> She has, more than anyone else I know, the technique of personal democracy and the art of making group irreconcilables meet as individuals to discover their common denominators. . . . One reason for her great radiation of personal democracy is her impartial hatred of any brand of prejudice; she knows that, psychologically, it is all of one piece, and that whether racial, religious, national, of class, caste, or sex, it is the same evil genius underlying most of our social misunderstandings and strife.

Throughout her career, McDowell had been politically active, involving herself in every municipal campaign, always in support of the reform candidate whose views seemed closest to her own vision of social betterment. In 1916, she had mounted her own campaign for county commissioner, running in tandem with Harriet Vittum, the head resident of the Northwestern University Settlement. *The Chicago Tribune* labeled the ticket the "Gold Dust Twins" after a popular cleaning agent and caricatured the two as scrubwomen, one with soap and bucket, the other with mop, a cartoon that did in fact capture the essence of their platform. But their campaign against widespread political graft was undercut by the issue of woman's suffrage, and a court ruling denying women the right to vote in that election meant the defeat of the Gold Dust Twins.

Then in the spring of 1923, a reform ticket swept the municipal election, and the new mayor appointed McDowell commissioner of the Department of Public Welfare. That department had fallen into disrepute in earlier days, a victim of the spoils system, and was mistrusted by all who most needed it. The Department of Public Welfare was said to be the "most useless on the municipal payroll." McDowell took command with one part-time assistant, a stenographer, and no funds. She asked for an annual budget of $9,000, received $3,500, and set about to do $9,000 worth of work with that $3,500.

She established her department as "the city's fact-finding machinery." Her thrust in the service of the city, as it had been in the service of Packingtown, was reform based on research. She called together representatives of all the city's welfare agencies, organizing them into an advisory council. Her question to them was direct: What can this department do, inadequately financed and ill-equipped as it is, to be of greatest service?

Their answers brought the Department of Public Welfare to work in several different areas, most immediately in that of Chicago's transient unemployed. Chicago, as a railroad center of the country, was a natural focal point for migratory labor. McDowell's department established a clearinghouse for homeless men in the "zone of the unemployed." The lodging house was operated not only as an agency of relief, but also as an agency of research, a fact-finding tool. The house supplied the necessities of shelter, warmth, food, and bathing facilities, while social workers secured records on reasons for unemployment and possibilities for rehabilitation.

The department's investigations into the city's female crime problem resulted in a separate detention home for women offenders. Another investigation led to a campaign to encourage the use of fresh milk in the diet of the city's children, and the poor were provided with ice for refrigeration during the summer months. Her investigation into housing conditions of the city's most troubled minorities, the blacks and the newly arriving Mexicans, led to a major report, "Living Conditions for Small Wage Earners in Chicago."

By 1926 the Department of Public Welfare was operating on a $50,000 budget, and its former tarnished image was all but forgotten. However, a 1927 change of administration left Mary McDowell without a political base, and she found herself out of office.

She had, of course, plenty of other work to turn to. Through the 35 years of her tenure as head resident of the settlement house, she had been a recognizable figure in every major movement for social progress. She was active in the NAACP and the Urban League. An early advocate of woman's suffrage, she had served on the first national board of the League of Women Voters and continued to participate in its activities both on national and local levels. In 1903 she had become a founding member of the National Trade Union League, and she fostered its activities until her death. She was on the board of directors of the YWCA and traveled to Europe in 1919 under its auspices to assess working conditions of women there.

She was, she once said, "a member of every organization I know," adding quickly, "[and] I hate organizations." It was a characteristically humorous quip, though it hid a kernel of truth. Organizations tend toward impersonality, and Mary McDowell was hardly impersonal. "She was never a cold executive person," said one of her associates. "Her influence was not to be found in the offices she held, but in the human relationships she strengthened and the social mission she imparted to an organization."

World War I had increased her interest in internationalism. She was a strong advocate of American participation in the League of Nations and the World Court. She had made several fact-finding trips to Europe, both before and after the war, and in the course of her travels she had visited the homeland of every nationality represented by her neighbors back of the yards. She made her last trip to

Europe in 1928 and at that time was honored by the governments of Lithuania and Czechoslovakia for her service to their people in Chicago.

In 1929, at 75, she retired from the active directorship of the University of Chicago Settlement House, though she lived on there as "head resident emeritus." In 1934, in observance of her eightieth birthday and the fortieth anniversary of the settlement house, a festive party was held at the International House of the University of Chicago. Mary McDowell's fresh vibrancy and the strong rich current of her leadership were greatly in evidence that night.

But within a year she had suffered a paralytic stroke from which she never fully recovered. She died on October 14, 1936, just shy of her eighty-second birthday. Her will specified that she was to have only "the simplest funeral that will not embarrass my friends."

At a memorial service for Mary McDowell, her neighbors tried to express what the Settlement Lady had meant to them. Though all the speeches were brief and halting, they gave eloquent testimony to the impact of one life. And none was more eloquent than the brief line spoken by a proud old Irish woman who had known Mary McDowell from the early days on Gross Avenue. "Oh," she said, "how I loved that woman."

To memorialize the woman who had brought life and hope to the people back of the yards, Gross Avenue was renamed McDowell Avenue, and in 1956 the University of Chicago Settlement became officially the Mary McDowell Settlement.* The citizens of Packingtown and the Chicago press had bestowed many titles upon Mary McDowell: she had been the Settlement Lady, Fighting Mary, the Angel of the Stockyards, the Duchess of Bubbly Creek, the Garbage Lady, Aunt Mary. But whatever her title, she had been a majestic figure, moving through endless crusades with fervor and with humor. She was, as Jane Addams said of her, "God-driven."

---

* Because of its deteriorating condition, the building was razed in 1973, but the Chicago Commons Association continues to carry out the work of the settlement.

·~· *Annie Smith Peck* ·~·
Mountains That Mattered

*W*ednesday. *September 2, 1909. 3:30 P.M. Annie Smith Peck had reached the summit of her ambition. She stood now where no human had stood before her. But the mood was hardly a triumphant one. The situation was, in fact, so desperate that for the first time in her 58 years, Annie Peck knew fear.*

This moment, this place had been her all-consuming goal. It was a goal that had eluded her in 5 previous attempts on the mountain. But now the goal was attained. And how hollow the victory seemed.

The wind blew fiercely at her and at her 2 companions. She quickly took pictures of the horizon in 4 directions, wondering all the while if the camera could even record the achievement, for all the swirling snow. Gabriel shrugged off his rucksack and stooped beside it, fumbling for the hypsometer. As his frozen fingers closed on the instrument, he lifted it out and set it on the icy surface of the ridge. Annie moved closer to him, spreading her poncho to shield the candle from the wind. Futilely, the guide struck match after match. Each time a fragile light flared and died.

Wind, thin air, and exhausted lungs made communication all but impossible. Annie caught Gabriel's eye and gestured the hopelessness of any attempt at measurement here and now. If they had, in fact, just conquered the highest peak of the hemisphere, that would have to be established later. Right now, survival, not records, was Annie Peck's goal. And one she almost despaired of. The struggle to the summit had exhausted them, and Annie knew there were even greater difficulties ahead. The camp lay 600 meters beneath them in the saddle. The icy surface of the great glacial peak sloped away at a 60-degree angle. Steps had been cut in the hard-packed snow all the way up, but the steps were small—too small, she was certain, to afford a sure foothold on the descent, especially after dark. And dark was only scant hours away now. The climb up the steep rocks and icy slopes had taken 7 hours; how long would it take to retrace their steps through the maze of crevasses in the face of this gale? This day, which might have brought glory, could now very easily end in tragedy.

Conditions were growing worse by the minute. She had lost a mitten during the ascent, and even as she surveyed their situation, she frantically rubbed circulation back into her left hand. And Rudolf, the older, more experienced guide, had troubles of his own; she knew his frostbitten hands and feet would need immediate attention once they got down off the mountain—if they got down off the mountain.

At her signal, Gabriel repacked the equipment, and doggedly the climbers made their way back along the summit ridge. Pausing just long enough at the edge of the icy slope to check their ropes, they started down, each tenuous step taking them one pace farther from Huascarán's cruel north peak and closer to the tent that meant temporary safety. Slowly they moved downward, Rudolf in the lead and Gabriel anchoring them. Darkness descended and a small moon rose at their backs. Their own figures shadowed the moon's weak light and darkened the way in front of them. Unable to grip his ice axe securely with his numbed hand, Rudolf slipped once on the steep slopes. Annie, without crampons or studded boots, slipped several times. Each time, Gabriel held. Despite cold and fatigue, darkness and shadow, the party inched down the glassy slopes. Time was interminable, conditions mocked human endurance, and the terror of the nightmare gripped Annie.

Then she heard Gabriel's voice on the wind. "We're safe . . . you can slide if you want." Below her, Peck made out the tent. In a graceless glissade she and the 2 guides tumbled the last 30 meters down onto the saddle where they'd established their final camp.

Exhausted, they clambered into the tent, rousing the native porters. It was 10:30. There was no alcohol to light their stove, there was nothing to drink, and their food was frozen inedibly solid. Numbed by fatigue and cold, huddled in blankets in a tent she shared on a wind-swept Andean ridge with 4 dozing Indians and 2 Swiss mountaineers, Annie Smith Peck silently and stoically marked the passing of the day that had carried her to the top of that glacial giant, Huascarán, a personal achievement that would stand unsurpassed for almost 30 years. She had triumphed and she had survived.

What life course had carried Annie Smith Peck to that unlikely spot? This most unconventional lady had come from a very conventional background. Yankee to her core, she was born in Providence, Rhode Island, on October 19, 1850. She was the youngest child and only daughter of George B. Peck, a lawyer and coal dealer, and Ann Power Smith Peck. On her father's side she was descended from Joseph Peck, who had arrived in Massachusetts in 1638. On her mother's side she was a descendent of Roger Williams, who had founded the colony at Providence in 1636. But this family could trace its genealogy back even beyond the first American settlements to tenth-century England. From her earliest awareness Annie Peck had a sure sense of her roots. And she had a sure sense of herself.

The Peck home reflected the austerity of Puritan New England, but it provided a healthful environment for growing bodies and minds. That environment fostered the development of Annie's unique spirit and skills, although her conventional, orthodox parents never did approve of her unconventional adult career. The family home was a cottage built by Annie's grandfather in 1798 on Main Street, where the town ran into the country. Behind the cottage was an orchard full of trees for climbing; across the road the North Burying Ground provided an imaginative setting for outdoor play.

Annie was a spindly youngster, but her build belied her abilities. She loved sports, and her competitive nature prompted her to excel in everything she tried. She climbed, skated, swam, rowed, played tennis, rode horses; she defied her brothers to bar her from their games, for there was nothing they could do that she could not do as well.

Her parents saw that she was trained as well in all the skills expected of a properly brought up girlchild. Annie often had to forego the afternoon's games in the Burying Ground in order to sit under her mother's watchful eye learning stitchery and practicing the piano. Excellence was always her goal, and she became an expert with the needle and an accomplished pianist.

The fresh, physical buoyancy that characterized Annie's nature was matched with a lively, inquisitive mind. In school she was invariably the leader of her class. Her parents imparted their own great respect for a classical education to each of their children. But while the boys, like their father before them, attended Brown University in Providence, the course of Annie's education was dictated by the fact that she was a girl. She attended Dr. Stockbridge's School for Young Ladies and later Providence High School. At age 22 she received a degree from Rhode Island State Normal School. She taught briefly in Providence before accepting a position as preceptress at the high school in Saginaw, Michigan.

But Annie's spirit was unfulfilled. When she discovered that the University of Michigan was accepting women into the same curriculum as men she immediately applied there and was accepted "without condition." In 1874 she enrolled at Ann Arbor, determined to secure an education the equal of her brothers'. Four years later she received her degree; she had distinguished herself in every branch of study and was ranked first in her class. She accepted a position as instructor of Latin and speech at Purdue University while continuing graduate studies at Michigan. In three years she had completed work for a master's degree in Greek.

In 1884 she resigned her position at Purdue and spent a year in Europe, studying music and language in Germany and wandering the archeological wonders of Italy. During that summer, on a trip to Switzerland, Annie Peck chanced upon the Matterhorn, and a new interest crowded into her life. She gazed upon "the frowning walls" of the famous alp, mesmerized by its majesty, and vowed that she would one day climb it. But not that day, for though Annie had roamed the Adirondacks as a child on family vacations, she knew the ascent of the 4478-meter Matterhorn demanded a skill and conditioning she had not yet acquired.

And there was another limitation on her aspirations—a limitation she first recognized here and one that was to dog her the rest of her life. Mountain climbing required funds. To Peck the $50 investment in guides and equipment necessary to climb to the summit "seemed a good deal for a day's amusement." Still, her imagination and her sense of adventure had been fired. And Annie had set herself a new goal.

In the meantime she was achieving other goals, breaking other barriers. In 1885 she was the first woman student admitted to the American School of Classical Studies in Athens. She spent the next year in residence in Greece, studying the ancient land and its language, its archeology and architecture—and "climbing the little mountains that came in [her] way." It was an exhilarating year for Annie Smith Peck. When her scholarship ran out, she returned home and accepted a chair in Latin at Smith College in Massachusetts. But her appetite for adventure had been whetted. This sedate teacher of the classics was being irresistibly drawn to other worlds.

She began to give parlor lectures to augment her salary and to gather funds for travel. Before genteel audiences she spoke about Greek and Roman culture, illustrating her lectures with slides made from pictures she'd taken on her travels and shown on a stereopticon.

She was an extremely interesting and popular speaker, and her lectures began to attract notice. Within a few years she was no longer teaching, but was supporting herself and her wanderlust by lecturing before college audiences, art institutes, and geographical societies. She commanded a fee of $125 for a series of 3 lectures and $50 for a single lecture. Her broadsides advertised her as "a profound classical scholar, a distinguished archeologist, and an accomplished musician." But more and more her interest focused on the mountains.

In 1888, with her oldest brother, George, a bachelor physician and the only member of her family who did not look askance on her activities, she climbed Mount Shasta, a 4300-meter peak in California. Shasta she called "the solitary peak," and there she experienced altitude sickness for the first and the only time in her life. It was her first important climb; she was 38 years old. She wrote that she found the "exercise of mountain climbing delightful and invigorating. The joy in the exhilarating atmosphere . . . must be felt to be understood. No one is acquainted with mountains who sees them only from valleys."

In the next 7 years she climbed in Yosemite and Yellowstone and, closer to home, in New England, where she explored the White Mountains of New Hampshire, in one day's tramp traversing all 9 peaks of the Presidential Range.

She was in Austria the summer of 1895 to do an article for *Century Magazine* on the passion play being given that year at Voder-Thiersee. Ten years had passed since she had first been entranced by the brooding presence of the Matterhorn. Now that she was right next door to Switzerland and had the skill, the time, and the money to attempt an ascent, why shouldn't she?

Up to that time she had never thought of mountain climbing as anything more than an amusement, but she realized that as long as she was going to climb the Matterhorn, she "might as well make it useful. . . ." It would, after all, make a very interesting subject for the lecture circuit.

And it did. Though Annie Smith Peck was not the first person, nor even the first woman, to climb the fabled peak, her accomplishment nonetheless drew worldwide notice. For the daring Miss Peck made her climb in knickerbockers, a hip-length tunic, and stout boots, with a jaunty canvas hat secured to her head by means of a veil tied under her chin. Her very outfit added an element of recklessness to her feat. At that time the few women who enjoyed mountain climbing did so in skirts, in deference to Victorian sensitivities. "Women will declare," Annie wrote later in defense of her action and her outfit, "that a skirt is no hindrance to their locomotion. This is obviously absurd. . . . I dare assert that knickerbockers are not only more comfortable, but more becoming, whether to the stout or the slender figure."

Her exploits brought fame and notoriety. She was now a national figure and an alpinist in earnest. She was also 45 years old, unmarried, and rootless, free to seize every opportunity for adventure. She was, by nature, well-equipped for the life she embraced. She was proud, she was determined. She was an individual who valued her independence and asserted her rights, daring to attempt what the world said a woman could not, should not, do. She was possessed of an indomitable will and a steely determination to achieve, no matter what the opinion of others.

She never hesitated to match herself against obstacles or odds, but she insisted, "I do not do foolhardy things and take risks." As she explained it,

> People think . . . that I do, but they are things that I know that I can do. . . . The difficulties and dangers of mountaineering are greatly overestimated by those who have no practical acquaintance with this form of athletics. All it takes is a sure foot and steady head in high places, a sound heart, strong lungs, and good nerves.

Admittedly not all upon whom she would have to depend shared her offhand assessment of the skills necessary to challenge a mountain. She would often be frustrated that the will and the courage of others did not match her own. But those days of disappointment were still ahead of her. Now, flushed with fame and success, she embarked on a full-time career as world traveler and mountain climber, raising the needed funds through her activities as a freelance writer and public lecturer.

She had climbed the Matterhorn; next came other peaks in the

Alps and the Dolomites—Breithorn, Grossglockner, the Funffin girspitze, and Jungfrau, all classic climbs. And all these mountain-climbing experiences were duly transformed into very popular lectures.

Annie Smith Peck was invariably a startling figure to those who filled the lecture halls to hear the stories of her adventures. Her audiences could hardly accept the petite person who strode on stage in stylish feminine attire as the woman who scaled precipitous rock and glacial slopes. She was barely 5 feet tall, a diminutive figure, yet she commanded her audiences with a powerful stage presence. A reviewer wrote of one of her lectures:

> She spoke of glaciers and crevasses, of snow fields and mountain storms with the familiarity of one who might be describing a trip through the subway . . . of her own city. What one admires, even more than the modesty of the climber's recital, is the wonderful pluck of this intrepid lady, to which her narrative bears testimony.

The narrative was invariably delivered in a captivating manner; everyone commented on the beauty of her voice. And the narrative was always accompanied by breathtaking views of the countries she'd visited and the heights she'd claimed. Annie Peck's fame grew, and with it, her ambition. Having climbed the European peaks of interest, she now looked to conquer the heights of her own hemisphere. In 1897 the *New York World* financed her ascent of Mount Popocatépetl, an active volcano in southern Mexico. When she cabled the news of her conquest she added a postscript to the wire: "As it turned out, it wasn't a difficult climb at all and a nice little boy reached the summit before I did." Popocatépetl's peak was 5452 meters in elevation; it represented the highest altitude ever climbed by a woman; the editors of the *World* decided to delete the last line of Peck's report from the story they printed.

Next, she climbed 5747-meter Mount Orizaba, Popocatépetl's neighbor, thus breaking her own world's record. "The peak utters a challenge. The climber responds," Annie Peck said once in attempting to explain the vocation of mountaineering. And from her Mexican expedition onward, she responded with a rucksack full of borrowed scientific instruments. Her expeditions gathered meteorological, geological, and topographical information for government agencies and universities alike.

By 1900 Annie Smith Peck had climbed 20 major mountains of the world and was a fully accepted member of the fraternity of alpinists. In that year she was a delegate for the United States to the International Congress of Alpinism in Paris. In 1902 she became a charter member of the American Alpine Club, formed by and for the country's mountaineering elite. She had achieved the heights of a male-dominated field in a male-dominated age.

Her goal now was "to do a little genuine exploration, to conquer a virgin peak, to attain some height where no man had previously stood." In her search for such a peak she turned to South America and the Andes. There in that massive range were snow-clad mountains that overshadowed Mount McKinley, mountains beside which the Alps were foothills. Almost anywhere in the Andes one was on untrodden ground. Engineers had explored certain areas to find the best routes for railroads, and miners had penetrated here and there in search of precious metals, but the entire area was sparsely settled and travelers were few.

Most of the mountains had no names, or names that varied from village to village. Their heights were largely a matter of speculation, for very few peaks had actually been climbed and measured. And methods of measurement were not always accurate. The barometers and hypsometers used in those days were crude instruments, and triangulation could give varying figures. Speculation as to the highest peak, not only of the hemisphere, but of the world, ran rampant.

The turn of the century marked a new age of exploration and adventure, with Peary, Amundsen, and Scott racing for the poles and every climber looking for the mountain that would exceed the world's record. It was almost universally accepted among the fraternity of alpinists that W. W. Graham held the world's climbing record of 7320 meters attained on Kabru in the Himalayas in 1883, and that Fitzgerald, another Englishman, held the record for the western hemisphere with his ascent of Aconcagua, a 6960-meter peak in Argentina, in 1897.

Well-founded rumor reached Peck that the peak of Mount Il-lampu in Bolivia was 6500 to 7500 meters above sea level. And it was yet unclimbed. It might prove, Annie believed, to be the loftiest peak of the hemisphere, perhaps of the world. She decided upon the ascent of Illampu. The fact that Sir Martin Conway, the fabled British climber, had tried and failed to reach its summit added zest to her project. But even for a person of Annie's indomitable will, the decision to attempt the ascent of a peak in the Andes invited some awesome problems. Mountain-climbing expeditions were major logistical efforts requiring strong financial backing. Other noted alpinists outfitted and commanded support parties of 100 or more porters and guides, with all the necessary provisions, equipment, and pack animals. Annie had only herself, her bamboo alpenstock, and an ice axe on which was burned "A. S. Peck, Matterhorn, August 21, 1895."

And climbing in the Andes would be much different from the art as practiced in European and North American ranges. Here the ordinary difficulties of climbing would be compounded by special difficulties caused by the extreme altitudes of the Andes. Such altitudes meant inhuman cold and an oxygen-poor atmosphere so thin it punished the lungs. One other factor pertained. Experienced guides served the climbers of the Alps and Himalayas; in South America there were no native guides. The superstitions of mountain lore kept the local villagers well below the snow line of the massive peaks.

Hence, in turning toward South America, Annie Peck had set herself a formidable task. "Some persons declared me insane," she wrote later in telling the story of Illampu, "others advised me to stay at home. To the latter I said I would if I had one." For, in truth, the peripatetic woman lived out of her trunk. When she was in this country she was invariably lodged in an apartment hotel in New York City. Her possessions were few and were easily packed and stored, as necessary. Shelves of books and a spinning wheel anchored her to home life, but did not get in her way when it was time to get up and go again.

Mounting her quest involved gathering funds. She herself estimated that she would need $5,000 to undertake the venture. By 1903 she had secured the patronage of a leading magazine and a few individuals, but was still far short of her real need. Undaunted, she sent for two Swiss guides, one of whom had served Conway on his attempt to climb Illampu. She also invited W.G. Light, a botanist, geologist, entomologist, and president of the University of New Mexico, to accompany her and share the scientific work of the expedition.

She equipped the party as carefully as her funds would permit. First, she exchanged her customary garb of prior climbings—the knickerbockers, tunic, and canvas hat—for an outfit more suitable for the Andean environment. At Admiral Peary's suggestion and with the permission of the Museum of Natural History she borrowed from that institution an Eskimo suit that Peary had brought from one of his polar expeditions. She gathered instruments for scientific observation, instruments for recording body functions as well as for measuring meteorological and topographical phenomena. This time, rather than a bulky barometer, she carried a hypsometer by which one could measure the temperature of boiling water and thus establish the height above sea level.

Peck also brought with her from New York the food on which the party would rely, food easily prepared and digested—dry soups, tea and cocoa, brandy and chocolate. She also carried erbswurst, a German sausage, developed as an army ration and containing in condensed form, "all the ingredients essential to strength and health." In Bolivia she added a good store of coca leaves to their supplies. The coca was a strong stimulant. "Chewing coca leaves enables one to defy hunger, thirst, sleep, and fatigue," she wrote. "[It is] excellent for use in emergency, but injurious as a custom, undoubtedly stupefying to the intellect. . . ." Annie herself chewed the leaves as she climbed and always provided them for her native porters.

The *New York Times* carried an account of the sailing of the S.S. *Seguranca* on Tuesday, June 16, 1903. On board was the party bound for the Bolivian Andes to attempt a feat never before accomplished. The *Times* reporter interviewed the lady who was leading the small troupe and found her quite "delicate in appearance." But this delicate lady flipped his question back at him:

What is my object in climbing [Illampu]? Well, it's archeological, geological, geographical, and topographical. The summit of that great peak, which may prove to be the highest elevation on earth, has never yet been reached. I go fully equipped at a season of the year that is most favorable. . . . I think that I have an excellent chance to succeed.

This was the first of Annie Peck's many cruises to South America, and though the name of the steamer changed with almost every trip, the itinerary and the routine remained fairly standard. The trip generally involved 5 weeks of sailing between New York City and Callao, the port city of Lima, with an interruption at Colon, where the ship's passengers were carried across the Isthmus of Panama by a 3-hour rail trip and boarded on ship again at Panama City.

Across the isthmus the travelers faced the twin threat of malaria and yellow fever, and as the ship plied the Pacific coast of South America, ports were frequently closed because of localized outbreaks of bubonic plague. Annie, ever the intrepid traveler, loved these cruises. She published accounts of them, giving her impressions of fellow travelers, of the discomfort of frequent shipboard fumigations to avoid the spread of the tropical diseases, and of the progress she witnessed over the years on that great construction project that produced the Panama Canal.

Debarking in Callao on this first of her Andean trips, Annie established the pattern of her subsequent expeditions. A day or two were invested in Lima in the gathering of luggage and supplies, after which the party moved by rail to the interior of the country, pausing for a few days' rest at the railhead city to become acclimatized, to gather the good will of the local people, and to make inquiries as to the availability of "stalwart" native porters. The last leg of the journey was made by mule or horseback to the most remote settlement from which the quest could be launched.

For her expedition to Illampu, Peck's party thus wended its way across Peru and Bolivia to the picturesque town of Sorata, above which for 4000 meters rose the massive walls of the mountain. Despite a very festive send-off from the village, well-laid plans began to go awry almost from the start. The obstacle to her success was one of which she would complain for the rest of her career. "I could climb," she wrote, "but managing . . . men seemed beyond my power. . . . Some of my more experienced married sisters might have done better." Always, the men she hired, assuming they knew more than she, were reluctant to follow her directions. Often, simply in deference to a male ego, she was forced to allow the party to wander one way when her instincts or her experience would have dictated another.

Now, here on the slopes of Illampu she experienced this frustration for the first time. Even Annie's indomitable will could not control the impatience of the professor, the cowardice of the guides, and the desertion of the native porters. The party fell apart. And Annie Peck's first attempt to find the apex of America ended at the snow line of Mount Illampu, 1500 meters short of the summit.

Dejected, she dismissed the guides but salvaged the season by exploring the interior, visiting the site of an ancient pygmy village and studying fabled Inca ruins. The antiquities that abounded here in South America matched in interest those of the classical world. And even though Annie's fame as a mountaineer now exceeded her reputation as an archeologist, she did not neglect any opportunity to explore either a buried culture or an unclimbed peak.

Returning to New York in late fall, she spent the winter and spring of 1904 seeking backers for another assault on the Andes. She had learned much in her first attempt, and she was convinced of the feasibility of her plan. On June 21, 1904, she sailed again from New York; this time her funds were more limited, but her ambitions were higher. She went unaccompanied; this time she would rely only on herself and such natives as she could find in La Paz whom she judged trustworthy. This time not only would she conquer Illampu, she intended as well to attempt another peak. For during her trip of the previous year, a Peruvian engineer had told her of a snow-capped giant in the northwest of his country. Huascarán, he said, was surely the highest mountain in the hemisphere, and no one had ever climbed it.

She retraced her route south, arriving in La Paz to engage a gentleman guide and four native assistants. Her equipment was much the same as she had carried on the first attempt, though she added one rather imposing item. In La Paz she bought a crude cross, which she'd been advised would pacify the superstitions of the Indians who feared to invade the mountain fortress of their god without a symbol of appeasement.

The entourage that wended its way from La Paz to Sorata that year was less imposing a cavalcade than the one Peck had led the year before, and its outcome was no more successful. Once they had reached the base of the mountain and begun the climb, she found herself again a hapless victim of the slow-motion nature of the porters and the domineering nature of her gentleman guide. Lacking only one day's climb to the summit, she was finally forced to accede to the cry of "impossible" from her assistants. Defeated once again, not by the mountain but by her inability to find an assembly of companions whose energy and courage equaled her own, Peck turned back to La Paz.

It was late in the season, but she decided to move on quickly to Peru, to survey the peak she had been told of. If Huascarán did in fact look enticing, she still had time to mount one attempt. Of her first glimpse of this remote area of the world, which would become as much her home as ever her native New England was, Peck later wrote:

> The Peruvian valley of Huailas and its immediate surroundings are unsurpassed in grandeur and magnificence. On the west . . . rises the steep and rocky ridge—the Black Cordillera; on the east the magnificent White Cordillera. . . . In this range . . . looms the pride of the valley, the majestic Huascarán. A saddle mountain . . . its two peaks rising several thousand feet above the seat between . . . and its summit a rock wall standing at an angle of 85 degrees, surmounted by a thick layer of snow.

In the mountain village of Yungay at the head of the Huailas Valley and nestled beneath this vision, Peck established herself in the home of the hospitable Vinetea sisters, who would welcome her back time and again in her contest with Huascarán. From Yungay she surveyed her mountain. There was a dazzling whiteness to the peaks and their massive lower buttresses. This immense glacier was so visibly and terribly cut by a multitude of crevasses that it seemed impossible that even the most skillful could thread his way through such a maze. Local lore advised an ascent to the summit from the eastern face. Accordingly, Peck gathered a group of porters and crossed to the far side by muleback. Although only intending to reconnoiter, the party actually achieved the saddle before impassable cliffs barred further ascent.

Annie Peck returned to Yungay. The season was well advanced, but she was flushed with the expectation of success. She dispatched a report for a Sunday edition of the *Times*, replenished supplies, regathered her group of natives, and set out for the peak again, this time climbing from the nearer, western slope of the mountain. The party made rapid progress. The group was the most amenable, the most intelligent Peck had yet climbed with, and her spirits rose, only to be dashed by the violence of a snowstorm that blew in upon them just below the saddle. The season had turned; it would be foolhardy to proceed. Peck took readings of her location and her elevation, planted her name and the date in a bottle, and retreated.

At the end of 1904 she left Peru for New York, encouraged by what she had found and what she had proved. She knew she had the skill to match this mountain; she was bound to put this proud pinnacle beneath her foot. Illampu was forgotten; Huascarán would prove to be the apex of America. In New York again, she lectured and wrote, desperate for the funds she knew would be necessary to conquer the mountain. In 1906 Peck led two attempts on Huascarán's summit, both doomed to disappointing failure. Obstacles of every description beset the expeditions. On the first attempt the porters struck for an increase in wages; on the second they refused to advance above 4500 meters for fear that they would be turned to stone by angry gods. Salvaging something of the season, she explored other areas of Peru, searching for the source of the Amazon, and she climbed other less challenging, unnamed peaks.

She had made 4 attempts on Huascarán; anyone of a lesser nature would have been discouraged. But Annie Peck was patient—and single-minded. "I never like to give up what I have undertaken," she once said. "It's not my custom."

And she did not give up her peak. By 1908 she had the backing of *Harper's Magazine* and $3,000. She cabled Zermatt, Switzerland, for the guides she felt were essential to her success. On June 29, 1908, with Rudolf Tangwalder and Gabriel Zumtaugwald, she once more sailed from New York, certain that she would now attain the summit of her glacier. The first assault that season was ill-starred from the beginning. Annie discovered the first day out that they had brought film of the wrong size. Rudolf, the older and presumably more accomplished guide, fell victim to altitude sickness, or *soroche*, and returned to Yungay. Annie, Gabriel, and the porters forged ahead. They passed the snow line and then for 3 days climbed through the midst of ice walls and yawning chasms; at last they reached the saddle; on either side were the steep slopes to the twin summits. At that point they made a determination. The south peak, though it looked to be a few meters higher than the north peak, also appeared to be all but inaccessible. The north peak would be their goal.*

But Gabriel was near exhaustion. He could barely lift his axe; Annie knew that if they were to climb to the summit Gabriel would have to cut every step they took. Their food supply was low, the winds grew stronger, and their feet colder. She was probably 2 hours shy of the peak when she aborted the climb. A party of full strength could attain the summit with minimum risk. There was another day coming. Annie could wait. They retreated to Yungay, rested, renewed their supplies, and now complete with Rudolf, the party set out again. But the few days that had passed had brought such a change in the weather that Annie began to doubt the outcome. The skies were cloudier, the weather colder, the mountain thickly veiled. They climbed quickly on the lower slopes, reaching

---

* Later measurement confirmed Peck's estimate, and the south peak proved to be 114 meters higher than the north. Thus, Peck's party did not achieve the true summit of Huascarán.

the saddle on the second day. Summit day dawned bitterly cold and with gale winds. Conditions were so treacherous that Annie would have waited a day. But the guides did not think the weather would soon improve and advised that they either make the attempt or retreat. Annie's choice was easily made, and the trio climbed into history.

Annie Smith Peck was, and is, the only woman to have made a first ascent of one of the world's major mountains, and the world rejoiced in the news that was cabled from Lima. The conquest of Huascarán was greeted as one of the most remarkable feats in the history of mountaineering. That this ascent had been made by a woman rendered it all the more remarkable. Because their observations at the saddle established that elevation to be near 6100 meters, Peck believed both the north and south peaks exceeded 7000 meters and perhaps approached 7300. Though she had been unable to confirm this by exact measurement, she cabled her estimate home, proclaiming Huascarán to be the highest peak of the hemisphere, and the world accepted the feat as a new record.

The Lima Geographical Society honored her at a luncheon, and the Peruvian government gave her a heart-shaped gold medal and later renamed the north peak of Huascarán "Cumbre Aña Peck." At the end of the year, she returned home to receive her honors in America. In all her accounts she proclaimed her belief that the summit of Huascarán exceeded 7300 meters and that, should future triangulations prove that to be the case, then she would hold the world's altitude record.

Such claims induced an old rival, Mrs. Fanny Bullock-Workman, who herself had climbed over 7000 meters in the Himalayas, to hire a team of French scientists, at a cost in excess of $13,000, to measure the Andean peak. When Mrs. Workman's team reported their observations, they assigned an altitude of 6648 meters to Huascarán's north peak and 6763 to the south peak. Such a finding preserved Mrs. Bullock-Workman's record as the world's highest-climbing woman and turned back Huascarán's challenge to Aconcagua as the hemisphere's loftiest peak. Annie was not only disappointed to hear the figures, she was outraged at the blatant display of such a magnificent sum of money. The controversy raged publicly for months, with both parties, and their supporters, using the letters-to-the-editor section of the *Scientific American* and the *New York Times* as an open forum. When the American Alpine Club studied the case and confirmed Mrs. Bullock-Workman's figures, Annie Smith Peck angrily renounced her membership in that august society. But in a gracious letter to Mrs. Workman, read at a news conference, she conceded to her rival the world's record for a woman climber, while reserving for herself the record elevation achieved by an American in this hemisphere. That record was, in fact, hers by right and she retained it until the day she died.

What lay ahead of her now? What worlds to conquer? After her descent from Huascarán, Annie had said, "While I hope to climb again elsewhere . . . I don't know whether I shall try reaching such great heights again." Now, having had her hoped-for record taken from her, she renewed her search for the highest peak of the hemisphere. In 1910, having read a book that claimed that Coropuna, the great volcano of Peru, exceeded Aconcagua in height by some 40 meters, Annie Peck prepared herself for another climb.

In June of 1911, at age 61, she sailed again for South America. Always an ardent feminist, she now joined 2 causes. In her baggage this time she carried a brilliant yellow banner, on which was emblazoned the legend, "Votes for Women." Climbing again only with native porters and this time in open competition with a team of scientists and mountaineers from Yale University, Annie Smith Peck reached 2 of Coropuna's 5 peaks and planted her banner on the higher peak. She had climbed and descended the mountain before the rival party gained the top. Though she had added the conquest of 2 more virgin peaks to her total, she had again failed in her ultimate goal, for by her own measurement Coropuna rose only 6425 meters above sea level.

This was the last serious climb Annie Peck made. But retirement was hardly her style. She simply turned her energy to less strenuous activities. She became first and foremost a leading advocate of Pan-American relations and spent the next 20 years touring both continents, addressing South American audiences in both Spanish and Portuguese, and American audiences in English. Whatever the language, her message was the same—she sought to foster an understanding between the peoples of North and South America and to extend trade between nations. She published an account of her Andean expeditions, *Search for the Apex of America*, and 2 other highly respected books, *The South American Tour* and *Industrial and Commercial South America*.

She had been one of the earliest advocates of woman's suffrage. As a teenager she had been sure she would vote by the time she was 50 or 60. She was in fact 67 years old when she cast her first ballot, and she felt it was a victory to which she had made a major contribution. When woman's suffrage was attained, she concerned herself with the repeal of prohibition and with other national, state, and local issues. Her frequent letters to the editor of the *New York Times* presented her views on a broad range of subjects, her stance invariably reflecting her very rugged individualism. The last years of her life she spent "worrying a lot about the Roosevelt administration."

She continued to travel—on goodwill tours to South America, and to Europe to indulge further in studies of antiquity. Blazing trails to the end, she completed a 32,000-kilometer air tour of South America in 1930, an 80-year-old adventurer seeking to foster better relations with our Latin American neighbors and to prove the safety and feasibility of air travel. Flying in a dozen varieties of airplanes, she observed from the air the same terrain she'd once covered on foot, on muleback, and by rail. And the new form of travel excited her as much as had the more vigorous forms of earlier years. She returned from that 7-month trip to write her last book, *Flying Over South America*.

On her eightieth birthday in late 1930, she was feted at a dinner at the Hotel Commodore at which she was lauded as a woman who had "brought uncommon glory to women of all times." In 1932, at 82, she climbed Mount Madison in New Hampshire. Though not approaching the heights she'd attained in other days and other places, this mountain had been one of her first and remained one of her favorites. It was her last climb. A year later she gloried in a *New York Times* editorial that celebrated the twentieth anniversary of the conquest of Huascarán.

In her eighty-fifth year she took one more trip—returning to the scene of her exhilarating year at the American School of Classical Studies in Athens 50 years before. She was a humanist, she said, who could not leave the earth without one more glimpse of the Parthenon. There she climbed the steep hill to the Acropolis. It was a symbolic act that recaptured the spirit of Annie's life and seemed to be an adequate summation.

Shortly thereafter, on Thursday, July 18, 1935, Peck succumbed quietly to bronchial pneumonia, alone in her apartment at the Hotel Monterey in New York City. Her remains were taken home to Providence and there interred in the North Burying Ground. That quiet ceremony marked the end of a bustling, fulfilling life. Calling herself one of the "energetic few," Annie Peck had once avowed, "My only real pleasure is the satisfaction of going where no man has been before and where few can follow."

In seeking that pleasure, she had gathered considerable fame. Indeed, her *New York Times* obituary called her the world's most famous woman mountain climber, a phrase for which Annie Smith Peck would have taken the editor to task, could she have written one more letter. For Annie Smith Peck had frequently disclaimed such use of the language. She was no more a woman mountain climber, she said, than she was a woman scholar. She was, rather, a mountain climber and a scholar, and those titles need not be qualified in any way.

·~· *Ida Wells-Barnett* ·~·
Militant Crusader

*B*ut why won't they go to the governor?" Ida Wells-Barnett demanded. "They must go."

"No," her husband said firmly. "They say the hearing will be just
another whitewash and there's no sense in getting involved."

Wells-Barnett angrily stabbed at the potatoes on her plate. She
was infuriated by what she had just heard. Despite Ferdinand L.
Barnett's fervent pleading, 2 influential men had refused to tell Governor Charles Deneen what they knew of a lynching in Cairo, Illinois.

With no protest from the sheriff, an angry crowd had seized
"Frog" James, looped a noose around his neck, hanged him from the
town's most prominent lamp post, then fired over 500 bullets into his
lifeless corpse. When one bullet cut through the rope, leaders of the
frenzied crowd had dragged the body up Washington Street, fol-

lowed by men, women, and children. Near the alley where the corpse of the white woman had been found, they had cut off James's head, jammed it onto a fence post, doused his body with kerosene, and burned it to a crisp.

"I can't understand it," she snapped, "a sheriff lets an enraged mob take an accused prisoner away to be murdered without a trial and the only black witnesses don't want to get involved."

"Can't you make them go, Pa?" asked 11-year-old Herman.

"No, son," the gentle man at table's head answered heavily. "There's nothing I can do to change their minds." Then, glancing toward his wife, he added, "So, my dear, it would seem that you should go to Cairo and get the facts to confront the sheriff. Your train leaves at 8 o'clock."

Ida Wells-Barnett looked up with a start, her fork frozen in midair. Then, recovering quickly, she snapped, "Nonsense. I couldn't possibly leave the baby." At the sound of her name, little Alfreda smiled at her mother. The other 3 children stared nervously down at their plates.

"Well," Barnett said resignedly, "you, of all people, know how important it is to gather the evidence, but if you can't go, that's the end of the matter." With that he left the table with his evening paper.

Dismissing the older children, Wells-Barnett retired to her bedroom, lay down to sing little Alfreda to sleep, and fell into a fitful sleep herself.

She was awakened by 13-year-old Charles. "Mother, Pa says it's time to go."

"Go where?" she asked sleepily.

"To take the train to Cairo."

"I told your father downstairs that I was not going," she said irritably. "I don't see why I should have to go and do the work that the others refuse."

The heavy silence that followed was broken at last by the boy's voice. "Mother, if you don't go, nobody else will."

As Ida Wells-Barnett looked up at her son, she thought of that Scripture passage telling of the wisdom that comes from the mouths of babes and of sucklings. Sitting up, she gave the boy a quick squeeze and said, "Tell Daddy it's too late to catch the train now, but I'll go first thing in the morning."

As she lay back on her pillow and thought of the day ahead, Ida Wells-Barnett knew that her son had unwittingly uttered the words that had been the controlling force in her life—"If you don't go, nobody else will."

Though Ida Wells-Barnett couldn't even recall when she'd first felt the impact of those words, it seemed to her as if her whole life had been lived under their weight. Born on July 16, 1862, she'd spent less than 6 months of her life in slavery, yet she was to spend the next 60 years questing after freedoms that the Emancipation Proclamation alone could not provide.

Her father, Jim Wells, had grown up in the little town of Holly Springs, Mississippi. A slave and the son of his owner, he had taken his father's name and been raised as his companion. While apprenticed to a contractor to learn the carpenter's trade, he had met and married Elizabeth Warrenton, one of the contractor's slaves and a woman already known for her culinary skills. For Ida, their oldest child, her mother's stories of the beatings she'd received at the hands of former owners in Virginia served as harsh reminders of the disregard some whites had for members of the black race. Her father hardly spoke of his slave days, save one angry outburst against "Miss Polly" Wells, the barren wife of his former owner. On the day Mr. Wells died, Miss Polly had ordered a public stripping and beating of the black woman who had given her husband his only child. That woman was Jim Wells's mother, and he never forgave Miss Polly for her act of vengeance. Only later did Ida Wells come to understand the full significance of his anger and to appreciate all the ramifications of that incident.

While these and other such practical lessons came at home, the Wells children had their first formal schooling in elementary and secondary level classes at Rust College, a school founded and staffed by white missionaries from the North. Her father served on the school's first board of trustees, and her mother attended classes until she learned to read the Bible. The Scriptures and the works of William Shakespeare became young Ida's favorite reading matter. The lessons she learned therein, plus the deep spiritual store that was her mother's legacy, were to be her strength in the crisis she faced in 1878.

In that one year Ida lost both of her parents and an infant brother in the yellow fever epidemic that swept over the South and claimed the lives of 304 people in Holly Springs alone. With her sister Eugenia now a semi-invalid, 16-year-old Ida found herself solely responsible for the rearing of the 5 surviving siblings. Armed with the education she had received at Rust and a determination to keep the family together, she lengthened her schoolgirl dresses and applied for her first teaching job. Since the job was in a rural school some 9 kilometers distant, she left the children in the care of others through the school week, returning home on weekends to wash and bake for the week ahead.

By 1882, her sister Eugenia had died and Ida had accepted a teaching job near Memphis, moving herself and sisters Annie and Lillie to the home of her widowed aunt and leaving her two brothers to work as carpenter's apprentices. While she taught in a rural school of Shelby County, Tennessee, she studied to pass exams that would allow her to earn a position in the city schools of Memphis.

On May 4, 1884, she boarded the train for her teaching job in nearby Woodstock, making her way to the ladies' coach in which she always sat. The conductor, prompted by the recent nullification of civil rights laws guaranteeing blacks the right to first-class passage, asked her to move to the smoking car. Surprised and angered by his orders, she refused. When he tried to force her to move, she bit him and attached herself all the more firmly to her seat, displaying the militant flare that was to characterize many of her later efforts. The conductor sought the aid of the baggageman and, to the cheers of white passengers, the two men forced her out of the ladies' coach and into the smoking car. Incensed, she got off at the next stop, took the train back to Memphis, and filed suit. The case was heard before a circuit court judge who had served with the Union army, and Ida Wells was awarded $500 in damages.

Three years later Tennessee's Supreme Court reversed the decision on the grounds that her intention was to cause trouble for the railroad, rather than to claim a comfortable seat for herself. Ida Wells felt the reversal keenly, for hers was the first case in which a black plaintiff had appeared before the court since the U.S. Supreme Court had struck down the Civil Rights Bill as a violation of states' rights. As she later wrote, she had "firmly believed all along that the law was on our side and would, when we appealed to it, give us justice. I [felt] shorn of that belief and utterly discouraged."

Through the years in which she was seeking to win equality and recognition before the law, Ida Wells was teaching in the Memphis public schools, pursuing a higher degree at Fisk University, and taking part in lyceum lectures and travel programs available to teachers in the Memphis system. She gained a reputation as a competent, conscientious teacher, yet she never really cared for teaching and was continually frustrated by the separate and unequal opportunities offered by black schools.

In 1887, spurred by a need to tell the story of her experiences with the railroad, she had begun writing articles for black newspapers, using the pen name "Iola." That very year she had attended her first National Afro-American Press Convention, where she was elected assistant secretary and named most prominent correspondent for the American black press.

Shortly thereafter and while still maintaining her teaching career, she had bought an interest in and assumed the editorship of the *Memphis Free Speech and Headlight*. An 1891 editorial denouncing the practice of hiring incompetent black teachers who were on intimate terms with certain members of the white, all-male school board cost her her teaching position and forced her to make the newspaper, by now renamed *Free Speech*, support itself.

She turned to neighboring cities and states, soliciting subscriptions and advertisements, and within a year she was earning a salary as a journalist comparable to the one she had enjoyed as a teacher. She loved her work and took her responsibility seriously, for she realized that the *Free Speech* was the only newspaper in the Memphis area that would publish the truth for her people. The "white makes right" mentality of the white-owned papers often made a travesty of truth, distorting facts to suit editorial purposes.

Ida Wells gathered the facts and wrote the truth, even when doing so meant attacking some of the leaders of her own race. She had been especially irked by the passage of the infamous "understanding clause" at the Mississippi Constitutional Convention of 1890. That law stated that only those citizens who could demonstrate an understanding of the constitution by explaining a specified clause were eligible to vote. Since black would-be voters were always asked to read and explain clauses complex enough to stump a lawyer, the understanding clause effectively abrogated the Fifteenth Amendment's guarantee that the vote shall not be denied on account of "race, color, or previous condition of servitude." When Isiah Montgomery, the only black member of the convention, cast his vote for the "understanding clause," Wells wrote a scathing editorial denouncing his action.

Because of Wells's passion and integrity, the *Free Speech* became a successful, respected, and feared voice for the blacks of Memphis. On March 9, 1892, Ida Wells was in Natchez, Mississippi, investigating a story when she heard the news that was to set the course of her life. Three of her Memphis friends—Tom Moss, Calvin Mc-Dowell, and Will Steward—had been lynched. They had been beaten, abused, and shot to death by 9 men calling themselves deputy sheriffs.

Ida Wells was devastated. Tom Moss and his wife Ann were among her closest friends. She was godmother for their little daughter. Why would anyone want to lynch Tom Moss? Like most people, she had always tended to believe the prevailing myth—that lynchings were reserved for black men who assaulted white women, depraved, animalistic men who gave blacks a bad name. But far from being depraved, Moss, McDowell, and Steward were 3 of the most respected citizens of the black community. They were joint stockholders in the People's Grocery Company, and their chief crime, Wells was sure, had been to prove themselves able businessmen and capable competitors of a neighboring white grocer.

Now they were dead, and their murderers were celebrated as heroes, not arrested as criminals. Wells went home to Memphis to mourn her friends and to expose the ugliness and the brutality of their deaths. In sorting through the insanity, she came to recognize the subtle horror of the crime. Lynching was treated as a laudable act, not a criminal one, because the whites who controlled the forces of law saw the Negro as less than human. Lynching had become a barbaric but accepted means of keeping the black in his place. And Ida Wells knew that by daring to expose this twisted truth, she herself would become a prime candidate for lynching. But speak she must, for who would speak out if she kept silent?

The editorials that flew from her pen in the next weeks roused the black community to action. Tom Moss's last words had been a plea: "Tell my people to go West—there is no justice for them here." The *Free Speech* echoed his words and advocated his advice. In the wake of the tragedy thousands of blacks left Memphis for Oklahoma Territory, guided by Ida Wells's articles on the opportunities that lay in that new land. Those blacks who stayed behind boycotted all white-owned businesses, and Memphis felt the effect as sales fell and trolley cars ran empty.

Though the newspaper's exposé of the truth about lynchings and its espousal of the black boycott infuriated conservative Memphis whites, no action was taken against the paper until Wells produced an editorial implying that some of the "rape" cases might well involve white women who preferred the company of black men. This time the *Free Speech* had obviously gone too far, and the editor of the *Memphis Scimitar* called upon whites to rise up and defend the honor of their women by seizing the "black wretch who had written that foul lie."

Away on business, Ida Wells remained unaware of the furor caused by her last editorial until she arrived in New York City to hear news of the burning of the *Free Speech* offices. Though her co-editor, J.L. Fleming, had escaped with his life, the mob gathered outside the burnt-out building promised to lynch both editors, should they ever again enter Memphis. Exiled and deprived of her paper, Ida Wells continued to fight Judge Lynch, this time as a freelance reporter. Black newspapers in New York, Chicago, and across the nation carried her articles, but the white papers whose readers held the power to stop the lynchings ignored them completely.

Despairing of gaining a white audience in the United States, she accepted an invitation in 1893 to make a speaking tour of the British Isles. In England and Scotland she found audiences who listened, spellbound, to her accounts of lynch mob brutality, newspapers that made those accounts available to the masses, and churches that vowed to censure American churches that stayed silent in the face of such injustice.

Ida Wells explained to her British audiences how a custom that had started as a swift means of keeping order in the West had become a means of keeping blacks in their places in the South. Soon after the end of the Civil War, lynching had been adopted by Ku Klux Klansmen eager to show what would happen to blacks who dared to vote. In more recent years, whites had lynched those who disputed the terms of a contract, those who fought or merely "sassed" a white person, those who set fire to a barn or stole a cow, or those who were just suspicious-looking. For all of these crimes the remedy was the same—swift and terrible justice at the hands of a mob.

Once carried out in the dark of night by men disguised in white robes and hoods, lynchings had become public affairs conducted during daylight hours and supported by prominent citizens, including newspaper editors, lawyers, ministers, and teachers. Special excursion trains were often scheduled, photographers assembled, and school children released early to see the burning, hanging, or shooting. Mutilations were common, and toes, fingers, and ears of the victims were sometimes dispensed to onlookers eager for souvenirs. While all of this was justified as teaching respect for the laws of society, it was, in fact, the ultimate in contempt for the law.

The lynchings were condoned by civilized people, Wells said, "because the world believes that Negro men are despoilers of the virtue of white women." Branding this belief "a falsehood invented by the lynchers to justify acts of cruelty and outrage," she presented statistics proving that not one-third of those lynched were even charged with assaults on white women.

And what of those relatively few men who were so charged? Why were black men punished by the lynching mob when the assault of black women by white men had never drawn such punishment? That was a question that had tormented her ever since she had first learned the full facts of her father's mixed parentage. It was a question that had confronted her anew each time her investigative "why?" had elicited the standard justification for the lynching of a black man. By refusing to accept that easy alibi she had, in case after case, managed to uncover the true reasons for the murders. Having presented those reasons in the form of irrefutable statistics, she asked only that "the figures of the lynching record . . . be allowed to plead, trumpet tongued, in defense of the slandered dead, that the silence of concession be broken. . . ." This was the message Ida Wells delivered in speech after speech to her audiences in England and Scotland, both on this trip in 1893 and on her return a year later.

This "slender little woman, with clearcut features" was a powerful and convincing messenger. According to the *Manchester Guardian,* her audiences were impressed with her "quiet, refined manner, her intelligence and earnestness, her avoidance of all oratorical tricks, and her dependence upon the simple eloquence of facts." The truth that she had not been able to convey before through white-owned American newspapers was soon being transmitted back to the United States by the London Anti-Lynching Committee, by the Society of Brotherhood of Man, by the heads of British churches, and by the editors of British newspapers.

But at home Ida Wells's message was still disparaged. A London correspondent for the *New York Times* wrote of "this coffee-colored lady" whose "sensational charges, unhappily true in the main, are very skillfully mixed with stuff I feel sure is not true." He and others urged that "sober-minded, responsible Americans" refute the accusations of this "octoroon evangel," this "slanderous and nasty-minded mulattress who does not scruple to represent the victims of black brutes in the South as willing victims."

Upon landing in New York City at the end of her first tour, she was greeted by a *New York Times* editorial warning the "mulattress missionary" that a black man had, on that very day, assaulted a white woman on the streets of the city, an event making it unlikely that her message of mistreatment of the innocent would find a very receptive audience on this side of the Atlantic. Undaunted, Ida Wells spoke at several churches in New York City before leaving for Chicago and the World's Fair underway there.

There was plenty to occupy her mind on the long train ride to Illinois. Attacks such as those made by the editor of the *New York Times* were harsh, yet bearable, considering their source. Harder to take were attacks from upper-class blacks who considered her challenging stance a threat to their own secure position. She had first noted this lack of racial unity when blacks in Memphis had shown no support for her courageous stand against incompetent teachers in their schools. Even her daring exposé of the Tom Moss lynching had been condemned by the wealthy upper-class blacks who had the most to lose by any actions or statements critical of whites. Embittered by their reactions, Wells had characterized such blacks as "Negro sycophant[s who] 'bent the pliant hinges of the knee that thrift might follow fawning.' "

Now, once again, she had heard blacks saying that she was "no representative of her Race" and that her stand did not represent "the intelligent public sentiment of the colored people." Most damaging of all was the assertion made by a retired American diplomat who called her "a fraud . . . [who] knows nothing about the colored problem in the South" and argued that "a reputable or respectable Negro has never been lynched and never will be."

Wells brooded over such attacks. She was well aware that they were indicative of the lack of racial unity that she saw as the major obstacle to effective reform programs. En route to the Columbian Exposition, she was especially mindful of the harm petty bickering could bring to the cause. She knew that the appointment of a black

woman to the fair's press board had been nullified when a group
of her own race had convinced the fair's directors that she was
unworthy to serve as delegate. Despite the pleas of Ferdinand L.
Barnett, founding editor of the *Conservator*, Chicago's first black
newspaper, the board had refused to reinstate the woman.

The loss of that appointment meant that noted abolitionist Frederick Douglass was the only black holding a responsible position at
the Columbian Exposition of 1893. And although he was one of
the most respected Negroes in America, he was at the fair as a
representative of Haiti! Representation of black America at the fair
was limited to some displays of needlework and drawings in the
Woman's Building and 4 small exhibits by black colleges. Blacks
were conspicuously absent as exhibitors and as visitors to the Great
White City, the gleaming white facade erected to house the major
exhibits of the fair.

The irony of exclusion of blacks from a fair conceived as a national celebration of American achievement weighed heavily upon
Ida Wells. The Columbian Exposition, held on the four hundredth
anniversary of Columbus's voyage of discovery, was, in effect, an
exclusively white celebration of white accomplishments. It was the
need to speak against this mockery of equality and justice that drew
Ida Wells to Chicago.

She went immediately to the Haitian exhibit, where Douglass
presided, ready to put into action a plan conceived before her departure for England. With the help of Douglass and of journalists
Ferdinand L. Barnett and I. Garland Penn, Ida Wells wrote, edited,
and published "The Reason Why the Colored American Is Not
Represented in the World's Columbian Exposition." During the
course of the fair, 10,000 copies of the little booklet were distributed
to visitors.

The tract pointed out to fairgoers that the first slave ships had
arrived at Jamestown a year before the Puritans had landed at
Plymouth Rock; it championed the role blacks had played in the
building of America, detailed their progress in the quarter century
since their emancipation from slavery, and denounced their exclusion from the fair. Nowhere, said the booklet, could one find exhibits

that celebrated the contribution of the black race to American science, art, and industry.

The booklet had its impact, and the fair board belatedly planned a "Colored Jubilee Day" in honor of America's black citizens. Ida Wells saw a "Jubilee Day" as insult rather than honor, and she was horrified when Frederick Douglass accepted the token offering. She bristled at the notice that 2,000 free watermelons would be distributed, arguing that "The self-respect of the race is sold for a mess of pottage and the spectacle of the class of our people who will come on that excursion roaming around the grounds munching watermelons will do more to lower the race in the estimate of the world than anything else."

Unmoved by Douglass's gentle reminder that "All we have ever received has come to us in small concessions, and it is not the part of wisdom to despise the day of small things," she boycotted the event and urged others to join her. Ultimately, she was to admit that her prideful stand had been wrong, for Douglass managed to carry off the day with dignity, using the spotlight it gave him to denounce the exclusion of blacks not only from the fair, but from full participation in all of American life.

Ida Wells had great respect for Frederick Douglass, but of all the black leaders she found herself more and more drawn to Ferdinand Barnett, the newspaper editor and lawyer with whom she had worked during the fair and upon several previous occasions. She had often told friends that she had no time for frivolous dating but was waiting for marriage to a man she could respect, a man who shared her views and her commitments. She knew now that she had found him. A widower with 2 small boys, Ferdinand Barnett asked her to marry him in 1893, but she waited until June of 1895 to comply, cancelling the scheduled ceremony on 3 different occasions in order to give public speeches against lynchings.

She entered marriage with a firm resolution never to allow her role as wife to interfere with her role as crusader. She was ready enough to help with the care of Barnett's 2 sons, but she professed no interest in bearing children of her own; her maternal instincts, she said, had been amply satisfied in years of tending younger brothers and sisters. Nonetheless, she fell readily enough into the role, bearing 4 children and calling motherhood "a profession by itself."

Believing that the mother who did not gain "control . . . of her child's early and most plastic years" might well despair of ever gaining that control, she gave up her position as editor of the *Conservator* and tried to limit her activities until all of her children were of school age. Still, she did not wholly retire from the scene. She took one baby to Washington, D.C., where she organized the national meeting of the Association of Colored Women's Clubs, later took another infant on a voter-registration campaign, and made many speeches while a nurse or friend kept a fussy toddler outside in a hallway.

During her mothering years Wells-Barnett helped found the first kindergarten in the Negro district of Chicago, championed the opening of the first black theater, and publicly protested the showing of the film *Birth of a Nation*, which, while heralding a new art form, also dignified the atrocities of the Ku Klux Klan. She raised the alarm against all instances of segregation, hammering on the irony apparent in the fact that blacks could enter, as servants, places from which they were barred as private individuals.

She raged against the implications of advertisements such as the one published by the Women's Model Lodging House, which promised to give accommodations to "all women . . . except drunkards, immoral women, and negro women." She joined Jane Addams in successfully protesting a move to segregate Chicago's schools, and she denounced the restriction of Negroes to the back of the bus and to the balcony of the theater and their exclusion from religious organizations such as the Women's Christian Temperance Union.

When she exposed the segregationist policies of the YMCA, several wealthy donors withdrew their support from that group and gave nearly $9,000 to the establishment of the Negro Fellowship Reading Room and Social Center. The center was designed to give blacks newly arrived to Chicago a wholesome place to stay, good books to read, and expert guidance in obtaining employment. Founded to combat the high crime rate among blacks, the center was staffed by the men's Sunday school class taught by Wells-Barnett. Even after a YMCA was built in the black area and the donors' funds were channeled back into the work of the Y, Wells-Barnett kept the Negro Fellowship Center open for those who, for any reason, were refused admission to the YMCA.

The views that Ida Wells and Ferdinand Barnett had shared before their marriage were strengthened by their union. If their views were all but identical, their styles sometimes differed. Ida was always the more militant. It was she who had bought a gun in the aftermath of the lynching in Memphis in 1892 and had written "I felt that one had better die fighting against injustice than . . . die like . . . a rat in a trap. I had already determined to sell my life as dearly as possible if attacked." It was she who had commended the blacks who set fire to a town in the wake of a lynching, saying "not until the Negro rises in his might and takes a hand in resenting such cold-blooded murders, if he has to burn up whole towns, will a halt be called in wholesale lynchings." It was she who had taught her children to meet "fisticuffs with fisticuffs" in the turmoil that ensued when the Barnett family broke the color line by moving east of State Street, and it was she who had warned the crowd of angry whites at her door that if she died in violence, she planned to take some of her persecutors with her.

But if Ferdinand Barnett's calls to action were somewhat more gentle, they were not less pointed. As early as 1878 he had argued the necessity for according the race the dignity it deserved, urging white and black editors around the country to refrain from the common practice of writing Negro in lowercase and to "spell it with a capital," and the next year he had reminded delegates to the National Conference of Colored Men that "White people grant us few privileges voluntarily. We must wage continued warfare for our rights, or they will be disregarded or abridged."

His sympathies were clear, and his endeavors drew his wife's constant support, even while she was engaged in battles of her own. Active in national politics and true to the party of Lincoln, Barnett was named head of the Negro Bureau of the Republican National Committee in 1900. Under a Republican governor, he became the first Negro to hold the position of Assistant States Attorney, a post he held for 14 years. In 1906 he ran for city judge, but was defeated by such prejudice as was blatantly expressed in one editorial: "The bench is a position of absolute authority and white people will never willingly submit to receiving the law from a Negro."

Ferdinand L. Barnett was equally supportive of his wife's endeavors. He knew that there were times when no one else but she could present the truth so convincingly. He knew that there were places where no one else but she would dare to go. It was for this reason that he encouraged her to go to Cairo, Illinois, in 1909 to discover and publicize the truth about the "Frog" James lynching. It was in this spirit that he supported all her activities—organizational as well as political.

Among the most militant members of the Afro-American Council, Wells-Barnett served as head of that group's anti-lynching bureau until she and her husband resigned their membership in the council in protest of Booker T. Washington's policies of appeasement. Her refusal to compromise put Wells-Barnett constantly at odds with Washington, whose preoccupation with the importance of giving blacks an education in industrial arts seemed to her a concession that an entire race could and should aspire to nothing greater.

In 1909 Wells-Barnett took an active part in the conference that led to the establishment of the National Association for the Advancement of Colored People (NAACP), though she was soon to be disappointed by that group's lack of commitment to action. Blaming the NAACP's problems on white domination of the leadership, she soon withdrew her membership, though she later lamented the pride that had kept her from staying with the group and wondered aloud whether she could have imparted a spirit that would have made the NAACP "a live, active force in the lives of our people all over this country."

Certainly, Ida Wells-Barnett herself was a very active force in the lives of her people. When race riots flared in post-war years in Illinois, Arkansas, and in Chicago's own stockyard area, Wells-Barnett called upon various political and social service groups for help, went to the scenes of the riots, and gathered the facts for the country's major black newspapers. When those facts indicated injustice toward blacks as the root of those riots, she called upon the government and upon citizen groups to right the wrongs she'd uncovered.

Convinced that racial discrimination made a mockery of the democratic principles upon which America had been founded, she never hesitated to take her case to the highest levels. In 1898 she led a delegation to President McKinley to protest the lynching of a Negro postmaster, then joined in the Afro-American Council's censure of the president when he did nothing to bring the lynchers to justice. As a representative of the National Equal Rights League, she made a fruitless appearance in 1913 before President Woodrow Wilson to ask for an end to discrimination in government jobs.

That year brought the fiftieth anniversary of the Emancipation Proclamation. Wells-Barnett wrote an article for a nationally circulated magazine in which she warned that as a nation we imperil the foundations of our government in denying blacks their legal rights and asked, "In the celebration of the fiftieth year of the Negro's freedom, does it seem too much to ask white civilization, Christianity, and Democracy to be true to themselves on this as all other questions? They cannot then be false to any man or race of men."

In 1917, as the nation geared up for its entrance into the war that was to make the world safe for democracy, many white liberals rallied to her call as she directed the attention of the public to what she considered a most undemocratic judgment. Declaring that a need to "placate Southern hatred" had motivated the federal government's condemnation and hanging of 12 members of an all-black regiment involved in a Houston, Texas, riot, she began distribution of buttons calling for national mourning for the "martyred Negro soldiers." Her campaign soon brought government threats of a charge of treason unless she agreed to stop dispensing her buttons. Her defiant answer put an end to the matter:

I'd rather go down in history as one lone Negro who dared to tell the government that it had done a dastardly thing than to save my skin by taking back what I have said. I would consider it an honor to spend whatever years are necessary in prison as the one member of the race who protested, rather than be with all the 11,999,999 Negroes who didn't have to go to prison because they kept their mouths shut.

With every passing year she found that she had less and less patience with those who refused to speak out against injustice. She had long been aware that the help of white liberals alone would never be enough to free her people from their bondage. Blacks themselves had to overcome their individual differences and wage a concerted, united campaign if they were ever to reach their goals.

As she spoke before women's clubs on local, state, and national levels, she urged women to strive for racial unity and for integration into national women's groups. But she was stymied by a recurring phenomenon; she found that more often than not, bickering among club leaders themselves and ill-timed displays of pride impaired the effectiveness of black women in their dealings with white women. Speaking before the Alpha Suffrage Club, the nation's first group for black suffragists, she told the women that only in Chicago had blacks received "anything like adequate political recognition," because only in Chicago had they demanded "anything like adequate political recognition."

Despite all her efforts, Ida Wells-Barnett did not live to see the nation's blacks gain true political recognition. Through the distraction of World War I and into the late 1920s, the fight for equality seemed to be hopelessly stalled. Lynchings and segregated housing, transportation, and education remained harsh realities,* and her frustration was heightened by the realization that there was no readily available written record of the struggle of the blacks for equality in America. No black leader had left a record of Reconstruction days, and "only the Southern White man's misrepresentations [were] in the public libraries and college textbooks of the land." Current generations of young people were totally unaware of the

---

* After 71 years of record-keeping, 1952 was the first year in which no lynchings were recorded in the United States. Unfortunately, there have been lynchings since that date.

nature and the extent of the effort she and others before her had made on their behalf.

To avoid leaving the history of these years unrecorded, she determined to set down her own experiences in the belief that "our youth are entitled to the facts of race history which only the participants can give. . . ." She began that task in 1928, dedicating the volume to the young people for whom it was being written. Though the work was almost complete at her death from kidney disease on March 25, 1931, it did not find a publisher for another 40 years. In the years between the writing and the publishing of that autobiography, the city of Chicago bestowed on Ida Wells-Barnett 2 significant honors. In 1940, the 47-acre South Parkway Garden Apartments, housing over 7,000 people, became the Ida B. Wells Garden Homes, and in 1950, Ida Wells-Barnett was named one of the 25 outstanding women in the city's history.

By the time Ida Wells-Barnett's *Crusade for Justice* was published in 1970, blacks had proven, at last, the truth of words uttered by Ferdinand L. Barnett nearly a century earlier: "Individual action, however insignificant, becomes powerful when united and exerted in a common channel." And though Wells-Barnett's lone stand had not been enough to bring about the widespread changes she sought, the beliefs she held and the tactics she used were the beliefs and the tactics that eventually led her people to claim most of the freedoms she had prophesied would one day be theirs—if only they would work together in their effort to claim them.

In 1897 journalist Norman B. Wood had written, "God has raised up a modern Deborah in the person of Miss Ida B. Wells." It was an apt analogy, for like the prophet Deborah, Ida Wells-Barnett urged her people to rise and arm themselves for battle so that justice and fair treatment might at last be theirs. And like the prophet Deborah, Ida Wells-Barnett was courageous enough to lead the way, moving into the heat of the conflict, going where no man or woman had dared to go before, setting an example that would only be followed years after her death when the activists of the '50s and '60s launched the nationwide campaign that culminated in the sweeping civil rights legislation of the 1960s.

~ Candace Thurber Wheeler ~
A Design for Industry

*C*andace Wheeler turned her back to the window and glanced around the room. In her husband's study they'd be surrounded by all the artifacts of the man's world; well, that was appropriate enough for the moment, but she wished she didn't feel quite so uncomfortable. She intended no invasion. It was a matter of simple expediency. There was just no other space in the house suited to her needs this afternoon in 1877.

"Strange," the handsome matron mused, "it's really symptomatic of this whole affair. Woman's place! It's a matter of establishing a woman's place. Where is our place? Well, we'll start here and just see what happens."

The sounds of the storm outside drew her glance back to the window. A fierce wind was whipping wet snow and sleet against the windowpanes. While her thoughts were diverted, a carriage had *pulled up outside the 25th Street brownstone, and she now noticed the activity its arrival stirred. "Thank God," she muttered as she moved to the door to admit several wind-blown, fashionably dressed figures.*

"I was wondering," she said over the bustle of greetings and wrap taking, "if you'd brave this awful city today. I'd thought of sending 'round notices that we'd postpone our meeting, but then I thought, This is not just a Saturday tea and I'll not treat it as such."

The animated exchange that welled from her callers in response to this remark was an obvious endorsement of her decision. Flowing with the tide of this energy, she ushered the 4 women into the paneled room off the foyer. She prodded the fire in the grate as the visitors settled into the leather chairs that ringed the center of the room. Turning from the fireplace, she moved to the mahogany desk and picked up a sheaf of papers.

"Well," she said, "I've been over this before with each of you. The very fact that we are all here means that each of us is committed to the idea. And Mrs. Lane," she said, handing a folio to the woman behind whose chair she'd moved, "has agreed to serve as the president of our organization. I think that all but assures our success."

As she lightly touched the older woman's shoulder, she noted the smiles of agreement that passed among the others. She moved on around the outside of the circle, handing each of the women a folio before she slipped into the remaining empty chair. Arranging her skirts, she settled herself, allowing each of her companions to glance quickly over the words she'd copied and recopied. Then she straightened in her chair and began again.

"What you have in front of you is my attempt to put some tangible form to this idea that's absolutely controlled me for the last few months. These are our goals as I see them. Now what are your thoughts? Can we clarify? Can we agree?"

For the next 2 hours the room was alive with the exchange of ideas. "It might be better if" was interrupted by "Yes, but . . . ," and "I wonder if that's realistic" was overridden by "I know where the perfect quarters are. . . ."

By 5 o'clock, as the storm was blowing itself out in the lowering dusk, the wave of energy was ebbing in the room. "Well," said Candace Wheeler, leaning back in her chair and studying the tablet on her lap that held pages filled with hastily scrawled notes, "this represents quite an afternoon's achievement. I think we may have changed a few lives here today—and not just our own. I think we should toast ourselves."

The mood of the room perceptibly lightened as she moved to the cabinet that held her husband's array of liquor. She neatly aligned 5 wine glasses on a tray, poured into each a splash of fine sherry, and returned to the women, who had risen and were now grouped around the dying fire. She held the tray in the center of the circle of her friends. Each woman took a proffered glass. As her gaze swept each alive, expectant face, Candace Wheeler raised her glass. "To the Society of Decorative Art," she said quietly. And 5 women saluted the birth of a new idea.

Though the Society of Decorative Art was a name that could have been attached to almost any club formed by a group of fashionable women in New York City in 1877, the organization that took shape at the Wheeler home that February afternoon was not just another social venture of the elite. The Society of Decorative Art was a business venture, a move to open the American marketplace to the talents and skills of women. As of the late nineteenth century, there had never been such an outlet, and Wheeler's idea, while mildly revolutionary, was a timely response to an increasingly obvious need.

"Women of all classes had always been dependent upon the wage-earning capacity of men," she wrote years later in recalling the circumstances of the day, "and although the strict observance of the custom had become inconvenient and did not fit the times, the custom remained. But the time was ripe for a change."

The agent of change was an unlikely revolutionary. She was almost 50 years old, a grandmother, a woman whose life to that point had followed a pattern typical of that followed by almost any female born in the nineteenth century. She was an unlikely revolutionary, but one whose earlier life had taught her the skills and aptitudes she would now use for the benefit of American women, American business, and American art.

Candace Thurber Wheeler was a child of pioneer America, by her own account "born early enough in the nineteenth century to see and realize all the great business of the settlement of America, near enough to the troubled beginnings to have . . . dreams tortured with happenings to early settlers." Born in March 1827 in a small settlement called Delhi in the Delaware Valley of central New York, she was the second daughter and the third of 8 children born to Abner and Lucy Dunham Thurber.

The Thurber family lived across the river from town on a small dairy farm that provided the family food and served as a school of industry for the children. Abner Thurber supplemented the farm income as a fur trader, buying skins from trappers and hunters and selling them to the New York market. "We were not only traditional, but actual Puritans," Candace Thurber wrote years later in her autobiography, "repeating in 1828 the lives of our pioneer New England forefathers of a hundred years before."

She recalled that her mother, "handsome and healthy . . . manifested all the human and practical virtues," while her father, a Presbyterian deacon, "belonged to the line of religious enthusiasts, the prophets of the world, who stand upon the mountaintops." The Thurbers were steeped in the traits and traditions of New England, and the principles by which the children were raised were all the laudable Puritan virtues.

Abner and Lucy Thurber taught these virtues by book and by example. As closely proscribed an existence as the Thurber children led on that little New York farm, they were introduced to a wider world by the guests who frequented the Thurber home. There were straggling missionaries, Bible salesmen, and temperance lecturers, visitors whom the Thurber children heartily disliked for the dour atmosphere and extra work their visits imposed on the household. On the other hand, the young Thurbers were intrigued by the frequent furtive appearances of black men who lodged with them, never more than a night or two, and then were quickly gone. It was only long afterward that Candace understood that the Thurber farm was a way station on the Underground Railroad and that these occasional visitors were runaway slaves on their perilous journey to Canada.

The family's abolitionist sentiments were expressed in other ways: The Thurbers wore no cotton clothing, since cotton was a product of slave labor, and for the same reason they used no white sugar. Rather, their clothing came from flax grown on the farm and spun and woven into linen in the home, and maple syrup, drawn from their own trees, was their happily accepted sugar substitute.

The early education of all the Thurbers was accomplished at home. It was a well-rounded education, for the home was a lively center of culture in both domestic and fine arts. From her mother Candace Thurber learned all the household skills. From her youngest years she was involved in the making of cheese and butter, the smoking and curing of meats, and the preserving of fruits and vegetables. She dipped candles and spun flax into linen. And she very early learned the art of the needle. In her last years Candace Wheeler still treasured a small sampler embroidered quite simply, "Executed by Candace Thurber, her age six years." Such were the beginnings of the woman who was to sponsor the evolution of American textile design.

Her father supervised all other aspects of her education. He taught his children their sums "in fox and mink and muskrat skins." In all of them he encouraged an awareness of and love for nature. "It is a great gain to learn the beauty of common things," Wheeler observed later when she was successfully translating that beauty into pieces of art. She and her siblings had learned that lesson early in life during long walks with their father, walks punctuated by frequent stops to study and sketch a wild flower or a weed or a stalk of wheat.

In Candace, especially, her father detected and encouraged a talent for drawing. He also nurtured her love for poetry, creating for her a morocco-covered notebook into which he pasted the newspaper clipping of any poem that caught his fancy. From that book Candace memorized the earliest published efforts of such poets as Whittier and Lowell.

The mental and moral standards applied in the raising of the brood of Thurber children were lofty and very difficult to achieve. An early biographer wrote of the upbringing of Candace and her siblings: "They were [expected] to be intelligent and obedient and industrious and kind to others, and truthful. . . . They were taught that life meant work and that what concerned the welfare and happiness of others was their business."

Though Candace struggled conscientiously to meet her parents' expectations, she blessed forever an influence that brought relief from the "monotony of our unnatural effort to be good." Her grandmother Thurber was a very vital presence in the household, and this grand old lady fed young Candace's imagination with impious tales of her own childhood and encouraged in the child the touch of daring that was to be a perfect complement to the spirit of doing good. Without doubt this grandmother served as the role model for Candace Thurber's life, and she wrote of her in the fullness of her own years,

I have never quite said goodbye to my grandmother, for she was not alone the wise tender merry old lady . . . she embodied the whole progress of life from a beautiful, buoyant, well-carried Puritan girlhood through a stretch of pioneer and bravely borne vicissitudes to a calm and beautiful old age. She was such a vital creature. . . .

As she moved into her teens, Candace Wheeler remained within her family's sphere of influence as she pursued her studies at the Delaware Academy. Then, on an 1843 trip to New York City with family friends, 16-year-old Candace Thurber met Thomas M. Wheeler, a young bookkeeper 10 years her senior who had served in the government corps of civil engineers, laying out roads, canals, and tracts of land in Illinois and Indiana. Adventuresome and "rich in worldly experience," Tom Wheeler exposed Candace Thurber to works of music, art, and literature that had not been a part of her Puritan education.

He captured her fancy and he captured her heart. They were married in 1844 and enjoyed the closest of relationships for the next

51 years, sharing, supporting, and encouraging one another in all their common and individual endeavors.

Tom Wheeler established a shipping company, and the young couple settled into their first home in Brooklyn, then a pastoral village separated from the city by the East River, crossed only by ferry. Children arrived, a daughter first and then a son. As Candace Wheeler later recalled, she had been well-schooled in maternal duties "by enforced care of a succession of baby brothers and sisters. . . ."

The Wheelers quickly developed a circle of friends who shared their interests in art, literature, and music, and they opened their home to the young artists and writers of New York City. Candace Wheeler later recalled being drawn more and more into a "set of people who did things—that is, who were creators, although we at that time were only appreciators," and she ultimately concluded that her "familiarity with the painters themselves, with their studios, their work, and their talk of art was a constant education . . . and when I came to its study personally I found that the way had been prepared by our companionship with these pleasant friends."

These "pleasant friends" included Thomas Cole, Jervis McEntee, and George Innes—painters of romantic American landscapes and members of what is now known as the Hudson River School of painting. Since art and literature traveled in company together, Wheeler came to know as well such legendary figures as Washington Irving, Edgar Allan Poe, and William Cullen Bryant. If not yet a creator, Wheeler was a very active appreciator.

In 1854, the tenth year of their marriage, the growing family and its changing needs prompted the Wheelers to look farther out on Long Island for a suitable homestead. Just outside the old Dutch community of Jamaica they bought some acreage, "a gently sloping meadow which ran back into acres of woodland." There they built a country home, which they called Nestledown, and which was, in her words, "to be the warp and woof on which most of the happenings of our after-lives were to figure."

After the move to Long Island, another daughter and son were born, and Candace Wheeler indulged her instincts for mothering, decorating, and gardening. Inside the rambling, roomy cottage, she devoted herself to those labors she was later to see as the commercially valuable skills of almost every woman—she wove and knitted, painted and etched. And outside the house she created in other ways. In her Quaker bonnet she became a landmark of Long Island, always to be seen either driving her Morgan mare Bessie to the nurseries of Flushing to bring home a buggy-full of saplings that grew into the great trees that shaded Nestledown, or puttering in the garden, designing that scene as carefully as ever she designed any on easel or canvas.

As the children grew and the family interests became more school and business oriented, the Wheelers eventually bought a second house in New York City, and the brownstone on 25th Street between Fifth and Sixth Avenues served for years after as the center of their city activities. These were happy, prosperous years for the Wheeler family, and Candace Wheeler later marveled that they were so little touched by "the great Civil War," speculating that "perhaps we were [too] young and absorbed in the progress of our personal lives. . . [to have] fully realized the horror of the war."

In the fall of 1865 the Wheeler family spent 2 years abroad. For Candace Thurber Wheeler it was a significant time. During a winter spent in Dresden, with the children enrolled in school and her husband absorbed in business interests, Candace Wheeler took art classes. All that had gone before—the childhood years of sketching the small beauties of nature for her father, the later association with the noted American painters—had unwittingly been a lifetime preparation for the intense education she now undertook. An instinct for color was her natural gift, and the knowledge of form and technique she'd absorbed in the conversations with her painter friends now helped her progress rapidly under professional study.

She later remembered that Dresden winter as having marked "a departure from a simply personal phase of life, for it was the beginning of preparation for work in the world, for activities which should affect other lives and fortunes." Over the next decade, both back home and during later, shorter trips to England and the continent, Wheeler continued to devote her energies to family and home, yet more and more frequently she was giving time to her own development and interests.

"There came a time in middle life," she later told an interviewer, "when it was borne in on me that [my own relative] freedom from home duties and . . . economic problems . . . [meant that I had] a definite responsibility to the public." At this same time, she saw as well "the great need among women for a work to do."

In 1876 she began to discharge the responsibility she felt. The direction of her life was focused by 2 events. Early that summer her eldest daughter died. Seeking relief from the grief that overwhelmed her, she had traveled to Philadelphia for the Centennial Exhibition. That trip proved to be the catalyst that moved her toward her life's work.

At the Philadelphia fair, Candace Wheeler saw the art and industry of the world displayed in celebration of the nation's birthday. There she visited an exhibit of the Kensington School of Art and Needlework, an English enterprise founded to support "the decayed gentlewomen" of London. Though Wheeler abhorred the phrase, she instantly endorsed the concept, for at the Kensington exhibit she saw the ordinary arts and crafts that typified the handiwork of women everywhere displayed as products of commercial value.

And why shouldn't they be so displayed? Why shouldn't a woman's accomplishments in the domestic arts be turned to account just as profitably as were the various accomplishments of skilled male laborers? Only custom weighed against it, and the custom was nonsense! Gradually, "in the midst of [the] sight-seeing and study" of Philadelphia, Wheeler conceived a plan and outlined a circular that would describe her vision of a new commercial opportunity for women. At home in New York she reviewed her plan and became convinced that, with the help of some energetic and influential friends, she could set in motion the machinery that would bring the idea to life.

And so on that stormy Saturday afternoon, February 24, 1877, she gathered her friends in the Wheeler home, and the Society of Decorative Art was established. The society's goals were to encourage profitable industries among women who possessed artistic talent and to furnish a market for their work; to accumulate and distribute information concerning various art industries; and to form classes of instruction in various forms of artwork so that "each worker could thoroughly master her work and gain a reputation of commercial value."

In keeping with the first of these goals, the group soon issued a circular announcing to the women of New York the proposed establishment of a "place for the exhibition and sale of sculpture, paintings, wood carvings, . . . porcelain and pottery, . . . tapestry and hangings, . . . lacework and needlework, which work shall be done by women." The immediate response was rather astonishing. Two hundred women applied for admission of their work to the showroom established in rented spaces at 4 East 20th Street. "It seemed as if every one of the contributing members . . . had a storehouse of articles already prepared for sale," Wheeler wrote later of the instant success of the society.

Within a year, under the guidance and encouragement of Candace Wheeler, there were similar societies in 30 other American cities and one in Canada. These societies marked the beginning not only of new opportunities for women in American business, but also the beginning of a significant movement in American art. Not coincidentally, Wheeler's goals began to change.

Disagreement as to the proper purview of the New York society grew among the original board of directors. The Committee of Admissions was constantly asked to accept items that did not properly belong in the category of art. At issue was the point of art versus utility, and Candace Wheeler's natural sentiments were with the liberals. She wished to see no distinction made between well-baked pies and well-turned pots. Woman's industry embraced more than the "fine arts," and Wheeler wished to provide a market for all the perfected skills.

Before the society's second anniversary, Wheeler had resigned to become a charter member of the Woman's Exchange, an organization sharing the goals of the Society of Decorative Art but accepting for commissioned sale objects representing broader fields of labor. The exchange flourished as quickly as had the society, and its membership and studios soon spread far beyond New York. Though a charter member of the Woman's Exchange, Wheeler did not take an active part in the daily work of the organization, for very soon she was fully occupied in another direction.

Louis Tiffany, the son of the world-famous jeweler, had approached her with a proposition that immediately appealed to her. America was being swept by a renaissance in art, a wave that extended beyond the studios of painters and sculptors and engulfed almost all the levels of society. Private citizens were newly interested in decorating their homes, and board members and elected officials were giving thought to the beautification of business houses and public buildings.

Wanting to turn this artistic impulse to commercial advantage, Tiffany proposed the establishment of a firm of interior decorators, partnered by people of special expertise. His interest was in the uses of stained glass; Lockwood de Forest would contribute his knowledge of carved and ornamental woodwork; Samuel Colman, a respected painter, was to be the firm's specialist in color and textiles; and Candace Wheeler was to lend the partnership her expertise in woven tapestries and needlework. Wheeler enthusiastically accepted the offer and herself gave the fledgling firm its name—Associated Artists.

Wheeler's enthusiasm stemmed, in part, from the fact that the proposed venture fed her own larger ambitions. This time her energies would be given over to something more than a quasi-philanthropic organization. Associated Artists was truly a business enterprise, an original and innovative industry. Further, as the woman partner in the venture she could demonstrate that "a woman's labor, if well-trained, was needed in the world and could not only make its demands, but find its wages."

Associated Artists opened its studio in 1879 in a rented loft on Fourth Avenue. The firm's very first order was for the drop curtain of the new Madison Square Theatre, and the project involved each of the partners—Tiffany designed the scene that would decorate the curtain, Colman had the controlling decision on colors, de Forest found the materials, and Wheeler supervised the actual execution.

It was in the execution of this work that Wheeler learned the lessons that were to be the foundation of a new art technique, "a daring experiment in methods of appliqué." She achieved the "large effect" she sought for the landscape design through the use of many different materials—velvets, plushes, and silks. Each material and shade was so employed as to give the tone, shade, and texture of oak, birch, and yucca, of clear sunlit foregrounds, of tangles of misty green, and of blue vistas of distance. The final effect was that of a luxuriant woodland. The curtain that was raised at the grand opening of the Madison Square Theatre on February 4, 1880, was, in essence, a painting in textiles.

That work drew other impressive contracts to the Associated Artists. The firm did the interior design of the New York 7th Regiment Armory on Park Avenue and the Union League Club House on Fifth Avenue; they decorated Samuel Clemens's home in Hartford and the Palmer mansion in Chicago. Perhaps their most public project was the refurbishing of the White House, a contract undertaken when, upon the assassination of President Garfield, Vice-President Chester A. Arthur refused to assume occupancy of that venerable mansion until the living quarters were done over to his own elegant taste.

Candace Wheeler had long believed that the American designer had a special facility for applied art and a greater interest in color than European designers showed, yet the American textile industry relied on imports in the manufacture and design of its materials. There were no original American designs in embroideries, textiles, or even wallpaper, and Wheeler later recalled that she "could not see why American manufacturers should be without American character any more than any other form of art. Art applied to manufacture should have its roots in its own country."

As her concern became more and more focused on the development of a truly American design in textiles, her workrooms in the Fourth Avenue studio of Associated Artists became the center of creative experimentation. Her designers applied "varieties of stitches . . . to varieties in materials." Always the design and the material were studied in reference to their intended use.

Her ambition was to capture the market from imported materials and supplant the European silks with the products of her own designers, and emphasis was placed on developing less expensive, better wearing materials for the American market. Cotton and woolen stuffs were worked alongside silk. Denim was brought from Southern mills and worked into designer schemes. New fabrics, experimentations in color and texture, were created. Within 3 years designs developed in the studios of Associated Artists were unhesitatingly adopted by American manufacturers and buyers.

But Wheeler's ideas for truly American design were not limited to textiles. When an international competition in wallpaper design was announced, she and her workers turned their attention to experimentation in that medium, with results that stunned the rest of the mercantile world. The top 4 prizes in the 1881 Warren, Fuller competitive design went to the 4 entries of Associated Artists.

The drop curtain executed for the Madison Square Theatre had marked the development of a new technique in embroidery. Wheeler and her associates continued their experimentation in that medium, for she sensed the evolution of a distinctly national art form. "My dream was of American tapestries," she was later to recall, and from the pursuit of that dream there evolved the Wheeler tapestry, achieved through a patented technique of embroidery, "which carried within itself art qualities supposed to belong only to painting."

When Cornelius Vanderbilt the Younger commissioned a series of these uniquely American tapestries, Wheeler utilized sketches executed by her daughter Dora, a recognized artist in her own right. Dora, who had worked closely with her mother from the earliest days of Associated Artists, sketched the great themes of myth, which her mother's crew then translated into fabric. The Vanderbilt tapestries—"The Birth of Psyche," "The Winged Moon," "The Air Spirit," "The Water Spirit," "The Flower Spirit"—were accepted as an American revival of a medieval art form.

In 1883, on the flush of such personal and national achievement, Wheeler channeled her energies into two new undertakings; one fed her domestic spirit, and the other her acutely developed business sense. The stirrings to return to the beloved country of her growing-up years had never left her, and now the Wheelers joined her brother, a successful merchant in his own right, in buying acreage in the Catskills. They called their settlement Onteora, or "Hills of the Sky," and Candace Wheeler supervised the building of Pennyroyal, a home that would claim them every summer hence. Eventually, the Wheelers and Thurbers developed Onteora as a retreat community that drew a close circle of family and business friends back to cottages and campfires each summer.

In the midst of the development of the home and settlement at Onteora, Wheeler also pursued a new direction in her business world. Four years after the establishment of Associated Artists, she felt that its department of design, embroidery, and textiles—her department—had become sufficiently important to be carried on as a separate enterprise. Since Associated Artists had, in fact, outgrown its original purposes, each of the artist-partners agreed to disband their joint venture and resume a separate practice of the arts, with Wheeler retaining the firm's name.

She and her husband bought a 4-story brownstone at 115 East 23rd Street and converted it into airy studios and sunlit workrooms. There the work that had begun on Fourth Avenue continued to develop, and, as she later observed, the fact of her being "in some sort a pioneer of textile art in America gave impulse to [her] activities."

All that Wheeler had envisioned in the founding of the Society of Decorative Art a scant 6 years before was accomplished in Associated Artists. She had set out to show women how to turn the creative, artistic expressions of their domestic arts into profitable endeavors, and she had established a market for their work. The accomplishment of these goals had but enlarged her original vision. When opening a market to "home industries" created new and different demands, Candace Wheeler had expanded her art and its techniques to meet those demands, combining art and industry in the design, manufacture, and embellishment of American fabrics that equaled those produced anywhere in the world. Her Associated Artists now entered into contracts with great American fabric houses, supplying original American designs to their mills. American-made fabrics won the respect of foreign as well as domestic buyers, and the work of American women became an exported industry.

Further, Candace Wheeler's dream of truly American tapestries was fully realized in the works that came out of the 23rd Street studios. Designs produced by Dora Wheeler for the tapestries woven by Associated Artists now found their subjects in the figures that had grown out of American literature. Wheeler tapestries that were hung in homes and in museums depicted the figures created by Hawthorne and Longfellow. And Wheeler carefully fitted the material to the subject—Evangeline was woven upon a coarse homespun cloth and Minnehaha was embroidered with beads and buckskin.

Candace Wheeler, now in her sixties, was at the height of her productive powers. She was an astute business woman, but she was also the artist and dreamer. The recognition of this rare combination of qualities drew for her the assignment that would cap her career. In 1892 the nation was caught up in preparation for the World's Columbian Exposition, a fair to be held in Chicago in observance of the quadricentennial of Columbus's voyage of discovery. The fever of development that had swept American industry and art since the Philadelphia Centennial in 1876 would be expressed in Chicago in a great display of national pride and accomplishment.

Plans for the Great White City that was to stand outside Chicago in 1893 called for a Woman's Building to be designed by a 21-year-old Boston architect, Sophia Hayden. The building would house women's exhibits from each of the states, and Candace Wheeler, named director of the New York Bureau of Applied Arts, was to oversee her state's contribution to the Woman's Building. Concurrently named color director of the Woman's Building by the Board of Women Managers of the fair, she was responsible for furnishing and decorating the building's library, a large room that was to house a "great army of books from the very earliest utterances of women down to the present."

Wheeler set the New York State exhibit into motion, then devoted her energies and applied her talent and experience to the library project, aware of the importance of creating an interior design that would demonstrate to the greatest effect the advance of domestic industries as a field of art. Under the circumstances, she found that a difficult task. "All sorts of incompetent women were placed upon my staff," she later wrote, "and the solution and decisions of our body of women commissioners, important and authoritative as they seemed when we sat in council, were merely thistledown to the real governors who held the pursestrings and ran the machine."

Despite these obstacles, the library was beautifully decorated, and its tasteful decor was a tribute to the skills of Candace Wheeler. The colors of the lake and sky outside the room's great glassed wall were reflected in modulations of green and blue. For the ceiling, she commissioned a mural, which her daughter painted on canvas in the New York studio, then shipped to Chicago to be installed in the room. Busts of notable women sculpted by women artists lined the room. The oak chairs and library tables with which the room was furnished complemented the dark oak of the paneled walls and of the bookcases on which were shelved the works of women of all ages. The library's interior design was an appropriate testimony to a new profession and its ultimate practitioner.

After the triumph of Chicago, Wheeler returned to New York and finished out the century in pursuit of the business of Associated Artists. She had long been involved in the process of educating others in her art, teaching classes for the Society of Decorative Art and for the New York Institute for Artists-Artisans, and serving on the advisory council of the Woman's Art School of Cooper Union. She now gave time to teaching a broader audience through the writing of articles and books.

In *Harper's Monthly, Ladies Home Journal,* and *Good House-keeping* she wrote of home industries and domestic manufacture, of the design of kitchens and the decoration of walls, of the use of antiques and wild flowers. Her technical articles were accepted in architectural journals, and she wrote 2 important essays that were published in *Outlook*, a contemporary journal of the arts and sciences. In both essays, "Art Education for Women" and "Interior Design as a Profession for Women," she advocated advanced education for women, maintaining that "It should be as much a matter of course for a woman to be educated with reference to a profession as for a boy to prepare himself by special study for his future. Present life demands trained labor from every member of society."

Present life altered for Wheeler in 1895 when she lost her beloved companion of 50 years. Adjustment was difficult at first, for, as she later wrote, "There came a time when I could no longer say 'we' and I found myself in a lonesome land where no one remembered that I had ever been young or called me by my given name." Ultimately, widowhood led her into a more relaxed mode of existence. In 1899 she entrusted the conduct of the affairs of Associated Artists to her architect-son Dunham and devoted herself to travel and writing.

The early products of her retirement years were 2 books celebrating her life's interests. *Content in a Garden* summed up the joys she'd found in bending nature to her own design at Onteora, and *The Principles of Home Decoration* stated the creed by which she had practiced her art. In the development of a garden or in the decoration of a home she declared that "appropriateness" to use and purpose should be the standard and that color should give the spirit.

At a party celebrating her eightieth birthday she confessed to her family that she was following a new whim. She'd purchased 40 acres of pine and magnolia in Georgia and was going to give a new setting to the winters of her future. She and a lifelong friend had purchased adjoining tracts of land, and she intended to indulge herself once more in the designing and building of a home of her own. In its own very individual way, Wintergreen, her home in Thomasville, Georgia, gave her as many joys as had Nestledown and Pennyroyal. Not that those latter 2 sites were now abandoned, for the grand old lady continued to bustle between her retreats, in each setting involved in the lives and activities of the 2 generations of Wheelers that now succeeded her.

Still handsome, erect, and vital, she wrote into her ninety-fifth year; *Yesterdays in a Busy Life*, her autobiography, was published in 1918, when she was 90 years of age, and still she did not pause long to live in the past. Three years later she published *The Development of Embroidery in America* and continued thereafter to importune her agent to find a house to publish other manuscripts she had produced. To her niece, her namesake, she wrote from Georgia that she intended to do a "rousing tract [for] voting women" and that she had "a vision of a sort of book called 'The Third Generation,' dealing with the race question—which is one of America's future problems, I think."

And she continued to practice her art. "I am painting like mad," she wrote home from Wintergreen in the winter of 1920, "beautiful rose and camellia and peach blossom pictures, for the benefit of the City Library. They are to be sold at an Exhibition and sale in March." The "rose and camellia and peach blossom" subjects of these paintings were products of her Wintergreen gardens. Here she continued to thrill to the joys of planting and harvesting, writing home that whereas in the gardens of Nestledown and Onteora she had been obliged "to earn [her] joys," at Wintergreen "they jumped to meet me.... and I wonder if I have earned [them]."

When, on August 5, 1923, at the age of 96, Candace Thurber Wheeler died in the New York City home of her daughter Dora, she left no doubt as to whether or not she had earned her joys. Her obituary in the *New York Times* called her "an artist and an author," but she had been far more than artist and author. She had played a crucial role in the development of a national taste in art, she had pioneered in textile design and interior decorating, and she had opened up a field of American industry to women.

Source Notes

Sara Josephine Baker
Baker's autobiography, *Fighting for Life* (Arno Press, 1974), was the major source for this chapter. A valuable overview is provided by Leona Baumgartner in vol. I of *Notable American Women* (Belknap Press, 1971), and supportive materials were found in the *New York Times* and in numerous professional journals and popular magazines. The vignette is drawn from experiences described in *Fighting for Life*.

Kate Barnard
Major sources for this chapter include an unpublished thesis by Julee Short (University of Oklahoma, 1974) and Margaret Truman's *Women of Courage* (Morrow, 1976). An excellent overview is presented by Edith Copeland in vol. I of *Notable American Women* (Belknap Press, 1971), and Keith Bryant's "Kate Barnard . . . Progressive Era" (*Journal of Southern History*, May 1969) gave useful background. Also of importance were numerous articles in the *New York Times* and many of Barnard's own articles, notably "Working for the Friendless" (*Independent*, November 1907). The vignette is drawn from Barnard's *First Annual Report, Department of Charities and Corrections, for the Year 1908*.

Williamina Fleming
Major sources for this chapter include *The Harvard College Observatory: the First Four Directorships, 1839–1919* (Belknap Press, 1971) by Bessie Jones and Lyle Boyd; Fleming's speech, "A Field for Women's Work in Astronomy," (*Astronomy and Astrophysics*, vol. 12, 1893); Solon Bailey's *History and Work of Harvard Observatory* (McGraw-Hill, 1931); Edward Pickering's memorial to Fleming (*Harvard Graduates' Magazine*, vol. 20, 1911); A. J. Cannon's memorial to Fleming (*Scientific American*, June 3, 1911); Fleming's obituary by H. H. Turner (*Monthly Notices of the*

Royal Astronomical Society, February 1912); and Grace Agnes Thompson's "Williamina Paton Fleming" (*New England Magazine*, December 1912). An excellent overview is presented by Dorrit Hoffleit in vol. I of *Notable American Women* (Belknap Press, 1971). The vignette is drawn from an incident related in Struve and Zebergs' *Astronomy of the Twentieth Century*.

Orie Latham Hatcher

Belinda Friedman's unpublished doctoral dissertation, "Orie Latham Hatcher and the Southern Woman's Educational Alliance," (Duke University, 1981) provided us with invaluable information, much of it garnered from the Hatcher papers housed at Duke University's Perkins Library. Hatcher's own works, notably *Occupations for Women* (Hitchcock, 1927) and "Virginia Men and the New Era for Women" (*Nation*, June 1, 1918), were most useful, as were articles in the *New York Times* and the *Richmond Times-Dispatch*. An excellent overview by Sarah McCulloh Lemmon appears in vol. II of *Notable American Women* (Belknap Press, 1971), and there is helpful background matter in Josephine K. Henry's "The New Woman of the New South" (*Arena*, February 1895). The vignette is drawn from articles appearing in the *New York Times* and from an anecdote related by Virginia Dermott Cox.

Leta Stetter Hollingworth

Major sources for this chapter include Harry L. Hollingworth's *Leta Stetter Hollingworth: A Biography* (University of Nebraska Press, 1943) and the December 1940 memorial edition of *Teacher's College Record*. Equally valuable were Leta Hollingworth's own books and articles, notably *Prairie Years* (Columbia University Press, 1940); "Comparative Variability of the Sexes at Birth" (*American Journal of Sociology*, November 1914); and "New Woman in the Making" (*Current History*, October 1927). An excellent overview is given by Victoria S. Roemele in vol. II of *Notable American Women* (Belknap Press, 1971). The vignette is drawn from Leta Hollingworth's account of her early days in New York City as described in Harry Hollingworth's aforementioned biography.

Mary McDowell

Major sources for this chapter include Howard E. Wilson's *Mary McDowell, Neighbor* (University of Chicago Press, 1928); *Mary McDowell and Municipal Housekeeping*, a collection of articles by

McDowell and her associates compiled in 1938 by Caroline Hill; Elsie Ziegler's *Light a Little Lamp* (John Day, 1961); and Mary McDowell's own article, "How the Living Faith of One Social Worker Grew" (*Survey*, April 1, 1928). An excellent overview is presented by Louise Wade in vol. II of *Notable American Women* (Belknap Press, 1971). The vignette is drawn from Harold Swift's epilogue, "As We Knew Her in the Stock Yards," in *Mary McDowell and Municipal Housekeeping*.

Annie Smith Peck

Major sources include material from Peck's own hand, notably *Search for the Apex of America* (Dodd, Mead, 1911), "Practical Mountain Climbing" (*Outing*, September 1901), and "The First Ascent of Mount Huascaran" (*Harpers Monthly Magazine*, January 1909). Many entries in the *Providence Journal* and the *New York Times* provided information. Laura and Guy Waterman's consecutive articles in *New England Outdoors* (May and June 1981) give excellent background, as does Berta Buggs's overview in vol. III of *Notable American Women* (Belknap Press, 1971). The vignette is drawn from Peck's account of the climb in an article for *The Delineator*, July 1909.

Ida Wells-Barnett

Wells-Barnett's own writings were the basis for much of this chapter, and many of the quotations used here are reprinted by permission of the University of Chicago Press from *Crusade for Justice* by Ida Wells-Barnett, edited by Alfreda M. Duster (© 1970, The University of Chicago). Also useful were F. L. Barnett's "Race Unity" and Ida Wells-Barnett's "Lynching, Our National Crime" from Philip S. Foner's *The Voice of Black America* (Simon and Schuster, 1972); D. M. Tucker's "Miss Ida B. Wells and Memphis Lynching" (*Phylon*, Summer 1971); and E. M. Rudwick and August Meier's "Black Man in the 'White City'" (*Phylon*, Winter 1965). An excellent overview is presented by Eleanor Flexnor in vol. III of *Notable American Women* (Belknap Press, 1971). The vignette is drawn from Wells-Barnett's account of the "Frog" James case in *Crusade for Justice*.

Candace Thurber Wheeler

Major sources include Wheeler's autobiography, *Yesterdays in a Busy Life* (Harper and Brothers, 1918); her *Development of Embroidery in America* (Harper and Brothers, 1921); her "Decorative Art" (*Archi-*

tectural Record, vol. 4, 1892); her letters held at the Stowe-Day Foundation, Hartford, Connecticut; Sara Dolton's *Successful Woman* (Schulte, 1963); and Madeleine Stern's *We the Women* (Schulte, 1963). An excellent overview of Wheeler's life is presented by Ms. Stern in vol. III of *Notable American Women* (Belknap Press, 1971). The vignette is drawn from a scene in Wheeler's aforementioned autobiography.

Index

political activities of, 115, 116, 117–119
and race riots, 117
religious influences, 103, 105
teaching, 105
and travel abroad, 116, 119–120
and unionism, 105–106, 113–115
University of Chicago Settlement House, 100–102, 108–120
and use of statistics, 115, 116, 118, 119
and vocational education, 111–112
and woman's suffrage, 119
McEntee, Jervis, 165
McKinley, William, 156
Madison, Mount, 139–140
Madison Square Theater, 170, 171
Malone, "Typhoid Mary," 7
Manchester Guardian, 149
Mary McDowell Settlement, 120
Matterhorn, 125, 126, 130
Memphis (Tenn.), 144, 145, 146
Memphis Scimitar, 147
Miss Belle Peer's School, 64
Miss Thomas's (School for Girls), 4, 5
Mississippi Constitutional Convention of 1890, 146
Montague, Helen, M.D., 87
Montgomery, Isiah, 146
Morris, Glynn, 78
Mortality rates, 7, 10, 18, 19, 115
Moss, Ann, 146
Moss, Tom, 146, 147
A Mountain School (Hatcher), 76
Mumford, Mary Cooke Branch, 67

NAACP, 119, 155
National Afro-American Press Convention, 145
National Conference of Charities, 33
National Kindergarten College, 105
National Equal Rights League, 156
National Trade Union League, 115, 119

Negro Fellowship Reading Room and Social Center, 153, 154
Nestledown, 165, 166, 175, 176
"New Woman in the Making," (Hollingworth), 89
New York Bureau of Applied Arts, 173
New York City
  Baker, 1–2, 5–22
  Hatcher, 66, 69, 72, 73, 77
  Hollingworth, 85–99
  McDowell, 105
  Peck, 130, 132, 135, 136, 140
  Wells-Barnett, 148, 150
  Wheeler, 161, 164, 165, 166, 167
New York City Department of Public Health, 6, 9, 10, 18, 19
New York Herald Tribune, 42
New York Institute for Artists-Artisans, 174
New York Times, 13–14, 38, 42, 59, 61, 73, 75, 131, 135, 138, 139, 140, 149, 150, 176
New York Women's Medical College, 5
New York World, 128
North Burying Ground, 124, 140
Notable American Women, ix, x

Occupations for Women (Hatcher), 75–76
Oklahoma City, 27, 28, 29, 39, 43
Oklahoma City Business College, 27
Oklahoma Constitutional Convention, 30–31, 32
Oklahoma land run, 26, 27
Oklahoma State Constitution, 30–31, 32, 33, 35, 42, 44
Oklahoma Territory, 27, 147
  See also Twin Territories
Onteora, 172, 176
Orizaba, Mount, 128

Packingtown, 100–102, 107–120
Palmer, Bertha (Mrs. Potter), 170
Peary, Adm. Robert E., 129, 131